Reading Voices

Resources in Education

Other titles in this Series:

Adventure in Education, Richard Andrews

Beyond the Core Curriculum, Mike Harrison (Editor)

Developing the Child with Down's Syndrome, Joyce Mepsted (in preparation)

Evaluating the Primary School, Brian Hardie

The Language of Discipline (2nd edition), Bill Rogers

Local Management of Schools, Brent Davies & Chris Braund

Managing the Difficult Child, Molly Clarke (in preparation)

Managing the Primary School Budget, Brent Davies & Linda Ellison

Managing Stress in Schools, Marie Brown & Sue Ralph

Marketing the Primary School, Brian Hardie

School Development Planning, Corrie Giles

The School Library, Elizabeth King

The School Meals Service, Nan Berger

Teaching Science in the Primary School, Alan Cross & Gill Peet (Editors)
Book 1: A Reader; Book 2: Action Plans (in preparation)

Time Management for Teachers, Marie Brown & Sue Ralph (in preparation)

Resources in Education

Reading Voices

Young people discuss their reading choices

**Fiona M. Collins, Philippa Hunt
and Jacqueline Nunn**

Northcote House

First published in 1997 by Northcote House Publishers Ltd, Plymbridge House, Estover Road, Plymouth PL6 7PY, United Kingdom.
Tel: +44 (0) 1752 202368. Fax: +44 (0) 1752 202330.

British Library Cataloguing-in-Publication Data
A catalogue record for this book is available from the British Library.

ISBN 0-7463-0687-3

Typeset by PDQ Typesetting, Newcastle-under-Lyme
Printed and bound by in the United Kingdom

With many thanks to Pat Pinsent,
for all her help and support.

Contents

Introduction   1

1   Teachers, the Curriculum and School
    – Key Stage 2   3

2   Teachers, the Curriculum and School
    – Key Stages 3 and 4   11

3   Home Reading   21

4   Networking   33

5   Gender Issues   39

6   Access to Books   49

7   Covers and Packaging   62

8   Serial Reading   69

9   Feelings about Reading   76

The Survey   83

Talking about Books   85

Survey Results   91

Tables and Figures   93

Books Mentioned by Children Taking Part in the Survey   110

Bibliography   117

Index   119

Introduction

The National Centre for Research in Children's Literature (NCRCL) at Roehampton Institute London has set up a wide-ranging study of the reading of children and juveniles, aged between 4 and 16, representative of a cross section of the population. The study looked at what young people like to read, when they read and why they read. Initially a pilot study of the reading of just under 400 young people was carried out and this was published by the British Library in 1994 entitled *Contemporary Juvenile Reading Habits: A study of young people's reading at the end of the century.* By May 1995 the first main part of the survey, of more than 8834 children, was carried out (published in June 1996 entitled *Young People's Reading at the End of the Century*); it is hoped that the process will be repeated every five years. The survey was carried out in a written format. Younger children (Key Stage 1) were interviewed by an adult and their answers were recorded in a survey booklet. Older primary age children (Key Stage 2) and the secondary age group (Key Stages 3 & 4) recorded their own answers in booklets. The whole process of the questionnaire was carried out anonymously, so that children of Key Stages 2, 3 and 4 knew that their teachers would not have any knowledge of their answers. As part of the whole project 2% of the children surveyed were interviewed orally by a teacher. This book is about the interviews of the older primary age children (Key Stage 2) and the secondary age group (Key Stages 3 & 4). A deliberate decision was made to exclude the results of interviews with children below the age of seven as they often change their minds and become distracted while being interviewed, so that, on the whole, their answers do not reflect accurately their opinions about reading.

The primary and secondary age pupils were interviewed by their own teachers. Each interview was recorded on a tape machine and these were transcribed. The pupils were interviewed in a variety of ways; individually, in pairs and in fours according to how the school could organise the staff. Once the interviews were transcribed the three co-authors read through them and decided that the material could be most conveniently grouped into nine main areas, which consequently form the basis of the structure of this book. Chapters 1 and 2 are divided in the primary and secondary age phases, and relate to what the pupils said about reading in school, what they liked and did not like. Chapter 3 focuses on reading in the home: being read to by a parent, reading privately and where they read. Chapter 4 investigates the influence that friends have on book choice and the development of a network. Chapter 5 scrutinises gender differences betwen boys and girls in relation to reading and book choice. Outside influences are then examined, and in Chapter 6 access to books is investigated. Where do children find books to read? Do they borrow from a library? Do they ever visit a bookshop? In Chapter 7 the role that book covers play in helping a young person make a book choice is discussed. Chapter 8 looks at books in series and considers why these are so appealing to readers. The concluding chapter, Chapter 9, gives some attention to feelings about reading.

The final section of the book gives the results of the survey and a comprehensive list of children's books referred to in the text and mentioned by children in the survey.

Throughout the book we have tried very hard to keep the pupils' voices at the centre of our writing, and to do justice to the variety of their points of view, even when the opinions of the same age group are presented. In each chapter we have tried to identify some form of development and progression, as well as to compare what the children say with some of the results from the survey and with current theoretical perspectives.

1
Teachers, the Curriculum and School – Key Stage 2

I think it's better in Miss R.'s class, because, like, Miss R.'s reading...she takes care of reading, and we do a lot of reading in that class. *(11 year old)*

Well I didn't read as much until I came to this school because we have a reading session at first, but when I was at my old school we only used to read when the teacher told us to, and we'd got time. *(10 year old)*

I like...well, at school it's good because you read, and when I get home I lie on my bed and read instead of watching TV. *(10 year old)*

When a teacher promotes reading in the classroom, children, as the above quotes show, are aware of it and like it. They realise, through the teacher's enthusiasm, knowledge and support, that reading is important. At Key Stage 2, all too often the rest of the curriculum swamps the teaching of reading, and also reading for pleasure. The 1990 HMI report *The Teaching and Learning of Reading in Primary Schools* found that Key Stage 2 children, deemed fluent by their teachers, were often left to their own devices when choosing books, and the 'higher' skills of reading were not developed. *English in the National Curriculum* (1995) encourages the use of inference and deduction when reading, and for most readers this will only develop through active interaction with the text. All readers, especially children, need to be actively involved in the text, they need to be engaged with the characters, setting and plot. In the primary classroom this can be achieved through discussion, prediction, role play and writing.

The above comments from these three 10- and 11-year-old children show how much children can enjoy reading in school, whether it is private reading or being read to. The latter, in the form of a class reader, is a particularly important routine to develop at Key Stage 2, as it allows for the whole class to share a common narrative, to have experience of the same story, the same characters and the same setting. It will also give the less independent reader a chance to experience a more sophisticated story and may encourage a reluctant reader to read more. Recently, a PGCE Primary student was reading *The Midnight Fox* by Betsy Byars to a class of 10- and 11-year-old children. During the second time of reading, the children were perfectly behaved (this was not normal behaviour) and totally engrossed in the story. After the third reading the non-reader in the class came with his own copy, that his mother had bought him, and other children wanted to sit next to him, something they had not done before. After finishing the book a reluctant reader who could read but usually didn't, chose another book by Betsy Byars as he had enjoyed *The Midnight Fox* so much! As Aidan Chambers (1991) states:

> Ideally, every child should hear a piece of literature read aloud every day. Certainly, no teacher should be regarded as competent who does not ensure that this happens with the children in her charge. She may not read aloud to them herself every day, but she makes sure someone does.

However, it is not good enough for the teacher just to read aloud daily to the class; an important point is that the adult must also enjoy the book, and be able to enact the story through the use of intonation; to bring the narrative alive. The enthusiasm with which the text is read is very obvious to the class, as this 9-year-old girl clearly states:

> I like it when you read to us because you make nice voices [teacher laughs]. But I don't like it when Mrs F. reads to us because she just, like, says it in a plain voice.

Reading in a 'plain voice' therefore can very easily put the children off the book. The choice of book is also an important factor to consider. Not all books read aloud well, so that the following questions need to be considered: Does the book have pace and flow? Will it hold the children's attention? Is it of interest to them? If the book has all of these qualities and is read regularly in a stimulating way, the children have a good chance of becoming engaged in the story. If, on the other hand, it is read only once a week the children may lose the thread, become disinterested and eventually find it boring.

The story chosen should allow for real engagement in the text, so that pupils can 'respond imaginatively to the plot, characters, ideas, vocabulary and organisation of language in the literature' (*English in the National Curriculum* 1995). The text should also have suitable gaps, so that the listener, and/or reader, can fill these for themselves. If the text has different layers of meaning this will give the child further enjoyment on their second or third reading. As well as these parameters, the books also have to be brought actively alive for children through discussion and written activities. These will engage the children, as the following discussion between this 11-year-old boy, 9-year-old girl and their teacher illustrates:

Boy – I particularly enjoy this book that the teacher's reading at the moment. No, it was a previous book. It was called *The Conjuror's Game*, and it won an award. I really enjoyed that.

Teacher – What about you Robyn? Are there any books that you've read in class with your teachers that you've enjoyed?

Girl – Also there was one which was...and I can't actually remember the name or the author...I think it was something like Willoughby White or something....

Boy – *Wolves of Willoughby Chase.*

Girl – Yes, something like that.

Boy – I remember that. That was good. I liked that.

Teacher – That's Joan Aiken.

Girl – And...because ... it was, kind of, sharp, and I think it was...well, there are some books, you can't describe them.

Teacher – Actually sharp's a good word for Joan Aiken, because she is very...she's a very inventive writer.

Boy – To the point.

Teacher – Yes, sharp. You can really feel you're there.

Girl – Especially with some of the characters.

Teacher – Yes.

Girl – Like the strict ones.

Teacher – Yes. Miss Slighcarp. Wasn't it Miss Slighcarp?

Boy – Yes. Miss Slighcarp.

This is a fine example of the way that children and their teachers can have a detailed and fruitful discussion about a particular book and its characters. The teacher in this situation did not take over, but she contributed and added to the discussion. The language used to describe the style of writing and characters extended the children's thinking. Through intervening on an equal basis the teacher extends the children, for instance by adding, 'Yes, sharp. You can really feel you're there.' This allows the girl to develop her line of thought in relation to particular characters: 'Like the strict ones.' Talking regularly about stories, characters and plot will help children to develop their critical powers, to differentiate between the stories that they like and be able 'to refer to relevant passages or episodes to support their opinions.' (National Curriculum 1995). However, recent research by SCAA

(*One Week in March*) on reading aloud at Key Stage 2, found that:

> ...most of the books listed are being read aloud by the teacher to the
> whole class and the readings are often used as a spur to other activities,
> such as children's own writing, rather than simply for enjoyment or the
> edifying effect of literature. The problem of resources is pointed up:
> classes only have one copy of the book. (*cited Times Educational
> Supplement*, 22. 12. 95)

Thus, although books are being read aloud to children they are being
used as a stimulus for other related work. In most cases when listening to
the story children cannot see the text, as the teacher has the only copy. As
illustrated above in relation to *The Midnight Fox*, children like to see the
text, not necessarily to read aloud, but to see what the words look like.

As more and more schools are becoming aware of this fact, they are
beginning to introduce differentiated group reading, with or without the
teacher. This allows children to become involved with the text and to
develop their higher order reading skills, which will benefit them when they
go to secondary school.

A further development, linked to the reading of a class novel, will be to
introduce children to new or different authors, show them different genres
and different styles of writing. The regular visit, as a class, to the school
library or the local public library allows time for browsing and discussion,
not only between teacher and child but also between child and child (this is
discussed further in Chapter 4), as this 11-year-old girl describes:

> *Teacher* –   Who suggested you read Judy Blume?
> *Girl* –   No one really. I just went into the school library and I saw them,
> and Kelly, she said she'd read them except for *Tiger Eyes*, and she said
> they were good. So I just got *Tiger Eyes*.

An author like Judy Blume can cover a class of children like a rash; once one
child has read her and talked about her to their friends, the rest follow suit
in reading her as she is a relatively easy read for most 10- and 11-year-olds.
However her appeal is not just in the simplicity of the text but in the issues
that she deals with, such as friendship, racism, religion and family life. If a
class is hooked on Judy Blume or another such author the teacher may
decide to look at the author in depth. Comparing the books, the content of
the various books, the style of writing and the characters may help the class
to analyse why the author is so popular. This will encourage the young
reader to develop a critical edge. The teacher's role must also be to

intervene, in relation to the reading choices of individual children, and suggest other authors once she feels that a pupil has read enough of one author. Some children may get 'stuck' on one author. It is important that they are encouraged to read a range of books of different genres, content and style. Sue Palmer, editor of the Longman's Book Project (quoted in the *Times Educational Supplement* 22.12.95) states, 'I am a teacher and I would want to help an able reader move on to something more challenging. It's my job to help them find out about other books.' *English in the National Curriculum* (1995) also states that pupils 'should be introduced to a wide range of literature, and have opportunities to read extensively for their own interest and pleasure'.

But how do children see their teacher's role in helping them choose books? In the Survey, the question, *Who helps you choose books... the teacher?* led to a mixed response from Key Stage 2 children.

	Never, hardly ever %	Sometimes, often, very often %
Girls	52.2	47.7
Boys	59.1	41

This is a sad reflection of children's perceptions of their teacher's involvement in reading choices. Breaking down the results by age shows further disappointing results. At Year 3, 50% of children said that their teacher sometimes, often or very often helped them choose a book; however, by Year 6 only 38.4% said they had help. Breaking down the statistics even further showed a difference between boys and girls. 55.1% of Year 3 girls said that their teacher sometimes, often or very often helped them choose books compared with 44% of Year 3 boys questioned; four years later there was still a similar gap where 41.6% of Year 6 girls, compared to 34.8% of Year 6 boys, felt that their teacher sometimes, often or very often helped them choose books. One wonders if the difference in relation to gender is related to the fact that the majority of primary school teachers are female and boys feel that teachers do not have the same interests or know the books that would appeal to them. Whatever the case, the most disturbing aspect is that only approximately a half of the children surveyed at Year 3 and a third at Year 6 felt that their teacher helped them choose books for personal reading.

Resources, of course, are an important factor to consider. In schools where there is a limited supply of books, or books that are old fashioned, there will be a problem in relation to their appeal to the child reader, as outlined by this 11-year-old pupil:

Well, sometimes I get them from home. I don't like getting them from the school library because there isn't really a big selection, and there is some books around the corner, and we're not allowed to get them unless we're with Mrs F... But I'm with her now, so I can get them, and they're really nice books. And they're about that thick.

To promote reading and encourage children to be enthusiastic about reading in its many forms, it is important to have a wide range of up to date texts displayed in the classroom and around the school. Texts, as outlined in the *English in the National Curriculum* (1995), need to be there:

- with challenging subject matter that broadens perspectives and extends thinking;
- with more complex narrative structures and sustained ideas;
- that include figurative language, both poetry and prose;
- with a variety of structural and organisational features.

Such books could include *The True Story of the Three Pigs* by John Scieszka, as an interesting alternative to the traditional fairy tale, told from the wolf's point of view, or *The Wreck of the Zanzibar* in which Michael Morpurgo's use of language and the change of narrative voice brings the story alive for the reader. A well resourced classroom with an enthusiastic teacher cannot help but engage the independent reader. The more experience children have of reading a range of genres, the more developed and sophisticated their spoken and written language will become, and the more they will be willing to engage in writing books for themselves, as this 11-year-old girl shows:

> ...and I make books myself. I've started a book called *The First Umbrella Book*, and I write about pixies. I really like Enid Blyton books, and I've got loads at home, and I make up my own stories. I like doing that. And I make a book that I can show my children when I'm older.

Blyton's is a particularly easy style for children to emulate, because of her simple vocabulary, formulaic structure and regular story lines. A great many children still become independent readers through reading the work of Enid Blyton, usually at the beginning of Key Stage 2. While it is important to move such children on to more challenging and varied texts, it is also important to discuss, with avid readers of Blyton, the sexism, racism and classism in her books, so they can evaluate her style and content at a distance. These issues are discussed in *The Power of the Page* (1993) edited by Pat Pinsent.

READING FOR INFORMATION

Texts that are read in primary school are not only fiction, but also non-fiction, such as reference books, information books, newspapers and journals. When studying topics in history or geography, children will be expected to research for themselves and find out facts from information texts, which are not usually written in narrative style. Sometimes primary sources of evidence are used, such as maps or documents from the last century, as well as computer or CD Rom programmes. In some schools homework is set and children are expected to find out information for themselves, as these 11-year-old children discuss:

Boy – I went down the library...sometimes I get books...just because we need them for school, like to do a project or something.
Girl – Like me and Helen Taylor last year, we did about Explorers as a topic and we found loads of books...
Boy – I did about Rome.
Girl – And then we're doing one this year...and it's really hard to find loads of books about it.

These children have obviously been encouraged to read a range of books about a particular topic, as quite often information books for primary age children cover only the minimum of information. By reading a variety of books and discussing their content, children will be encouraged 'to distinguish between fact and opinion and consider an argument critically' (*English in the National Curriculum* 1995). Once again, resources are a key factor; if there is not a range in the school for the child researcher to use, their critical powers will be underdeveloped. Children need to be able to compare different books on subjects such as the Romans or Explorers. The young researcher also needs to develop different styles of reading, such as skimming and scanning, to allow them to find relevant information more quickly.

Finally, while looking at teachers, the curriculum and school at Key Stage 2 one major factor has emerged throughout: the importance of the role of the teacher in the development of reading. As Aidan Chambers (*The Reading Environment* 1991) clearly articulates:

What is it that enabling adults, teachers, especially do? They provide, they stimulate, demonstrate and respond. They provide books and time to read them and an attractive environment where people want to read. They demonstrate by reading aloud and by their own behaviour what a 'good' reader does. And they respond, and help others respond, to the individuality of everyone in the reading community they belong to.

RECOMMENDATIONS

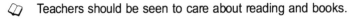

Teachers should be seen to care about reading and books.

A class reader should read regularly, with enthusiasm and feeling to bring the story alive for the children listening.

Books should be regularly talked about, in groups and within a whole class situation.

Classes should be well stocked with a good range of fiction and non-fiction books.

Teachers must be alert to the reading needs of the children in their class.

Teachers should make a point of helping children choose books according to their interest and the child's reading ability.

2

Teachers, the Curriculum and School – Key Stages 3 and 4

As soon as children move into the secondary sector, it is mainly specialist teachers who deliver the reading curriculum. This should mean that the knowledge and enthusiasm of the teachers are no longer problematic. Certainly, when graduates applying for a place on a PGCE secondary English course are asked why they want to teach, the most common reply is along the lines of 'I love Literature and I want to inspire pupils to feel the same.' Aspirations to improve the nation's spelling or encourage novelists of the future don't often get a mention but candidates become evangelical at the thought of spreading the good word about the joys to be had between the pages of a book. Experienced teachers of English may be a little more realistic about their power to influence pupils but many still see encouraging reading as a priority.

CHOICE OF BOOKS – KEY STAGE 3

Until the National Curriculum was introduced in 1990, English teachers had enormous freedom over the choice of fiction to study in their classrooms. Only for examination classes were there lists to guide choice. The first official version of the English orders began the change. Shakespeare became compulsory, as well as some study of other pre-twentieth century literature. There was also mention of introducing pupils to 'the richness of contemporary fiction', 'literature from other countries' and 'works which have been influential in shaping and refining the English language and its literature'. But there were no prescribed lists of titles or writers. Brian Cox, chairperson of the English group, explained why: 'There is such a variety of good literature available for inclusion in syllabuses that we want teachers to have the freedom to make their own choice of suitable books without our broad guidelines.' (Cox, 1991).

So during the time when the survey and interviews were carried out, there was an enormous flexibility for the teacher in the choice of text for close analysis in the classroom. The verbal reactions of pupils to these choices show how difficult it is for teachers to get it right. 'Boring, completely boring' is one depressing response from a 12-year-old boy when asked about the books read in class, but as he had already admitted that he hated reading, perhaps his comment should not be taken too seriously.

However, the dismissive comment of a 13-year-old who had recently read Robert Swindells' *Stone Cold* and Robin Jarvis's *The Whitby Witches* is more revealing. When asked whether she had enjoyed any of the books read in school, she replied:

> No not that much. I find them quite boring because there's no actual adventure in them. I like horror stories. School stories are just ordinary which I don't like.

This girl obviously wants her diet of school texts to mirror the choices she makes for her independent reading. Another girl of the same age is highly critical of the type of books chosen for study in school. First of all she makes a general point about the poor storylines and then she goes on to say:

> Some of them have got really bad endings...they don't end properly because they just seem to finish (laughs). I liked 'Adventure of the Beast' (Janni Howker's *Nature of the Beast*?); that seemed a weird ending.

A 14-year-old girl shows a similar attitude although she is prepared to be a little more tactful:

> *Teacher* – Are there any books you've shared with your year at school which you've especially enjoyed?
> *Girl* – Not especially, no. Some of them were OK, but I wouldn't have chosen them for my own reading.
> *Teacher* – But having been given them, do you appreciate that they are quite good, or do you still think they're rubbish?
> *Girl* – *Across the Barricades* is quite good.
> *Teacher* – *Across the Barricades*, yes.
> *Girl* – But most of them are quite boring (laughs).

Betsy Byars' *The Midnight Fox*, a favourite with many secondary teachers, is condemned as boring by several pupils. A possible reason for this might be that 12-year-olds feel that such a book belongs in the primary curriculum. Indeed, they may have already encountered it in their previous schools and felt the enthusiasm for it as described in Chapter 1. Secondary teachers have to guard against letting their pupils feel they have not progressed since moving up to the 'big school'.

Not all the comments from Key Stage 3 pupils are so negative. Nigel Hinton's *Buddy* is mentioned by several of the interviewees as 'a good book' and some choices appear to bridge the gap between home reading and school text. *The Nature of the Beast* by Janni Howker seems to be popular because it manages to mirror to some degree the private reading material of this age group.

> There's one we're reading just now. It's about *Nature of the Beast*...It's about those beasts up on the moors, and killing things. And I just like stories like that. Horror stories and things like that. (*13-year-old girl*)

Similarly, Gillian Cross's *A Dark Behind the Curtain* is praised by a girl of 12 because 'it's scary'.

Many teachers would argue that school texts should expand the range of literature experienced by pupils, not just mirror their own reading. Indeed, some of the pupils interviewed were prepared to see the value in being exposed by their teachers to a different type of book. One 13-year-old boy puts it like this:

> Some of the books you give us I've never really heard of. Some of them aren't the usual style that I read at home. But I like the one I'm reading now, about machine guns. That's quite a nice one. It's a good book. And I thought *Black Jack* was good. *The Guardians* I thought was quite good. It was different. It was certainly different, yes.

Further evidence that pupils can respond enthusiastically to books which are 'different' comes from a small classroom research project conducted in the Autumn Term of 1995. A teacher chose Philippa Pearce's *Tom's Midnight Garden* for the novel slot for two classes of 12 year olds. The teacher herself had some misgivings. She knew that the pupils' private reading was dominated by *Point Horror* titles and she had heard of other teachers failing with this modern classic. She decided to proceed because she wanted to teach a text she valued as 'quality' fiction. She hoped that she could encourage her classes to see that good writing is not just plot. As she explains:

> I described to them my own tendency to be addicted to plot, turning the pages of a book as quickly as possible to find out 'what happens' and missing out on detail and atmosphere in the process. The pupils instantly recognised the syndrome in their own reading and we agreed to take our time in order to appreciate Philippa Pearce's writing.

If one of the objects of teaching fiction in the classroom is to expose children to literature that they would not choose for themselves and then help them to see its value, this teacher certainly succeeded. At the beginning of the unit of work, some resistance was shown. Many openly admitted that they did not like the look of the book; they thought it would be boring. But by lively reading and imaginative strategies, the class was won over. The teacher did relate the book to the children's lives by asking questions such as 'Have you ever been sent somewhere you don't want to go?', 'Do you like skating?' – but she also concentrated on Philippa Pearce's writing.

> Philippa Pearce's imaginative world is stunningly detailed, and we played memory games recalling, for example, all the details of the garden. The pupils surpassed me, remembering the asparagus bed, the carving on the sundial, everything, and were very proud of themselves as a result. We also stopped to notice which of our five senses were appealed to – the smell of hyacinths, the feel of a cold flagstone and so forth. It was also worth pointing out the characterisation of Tom to them and ask them to role-play him. He is a difficult, prickly boy and they eventually enjoyed his complexity. They began to discuss how many of the characters in their own books are cyphers or stereotypes by comparison.

When the book was finished, the reaction of nearly every pupil was positive. A cross section of pupils was interviewed and they all expressed genuine pleasure in having studied it. Most striking was the reaction of a girl who confessed to being a horror addict:

> It was so different. I thought I'd hate it but it was good to read. I don't really like books like that but I liked it. I'd never have read it on my own.

CHOICE OF BOOKS – KEY STAGE 4

As pupils move into Key Stage 4, the pressure of examinations is a major factor. Novels, plays and poetry are now studied for a very real purpose. Teachers at this stage have to consult syllabuses, although personal preferences still count. The needs of the pupils are often more carefully considered. Questions such as, 'Will this novel allow the most able the opportunity to show their strengths while not confusing the weakest?' need to be answered. Many teachers feel that the tried and tested texts are safest. So *Of Mice and Men* is still being taught in countless classrooms across the country and *A Kestrel for a Knave* tops the charts as the most used novel for GCSE, despite the fact that it was first published in 1968.

Discouragingly, some of the pupils interviewed at this age are rather sceptical about their teacher's choice. One 15-year-old girl, who admits to quite liking Shakespeare, puts it this way:

> ...but the thing is that all the books that we've chosen, they're just chosen because there's lots you can write about them, not just because it's a good story.

A 15-year-old boy, while acknowledging that teachers give books to their pupils to educate them, sees it from the author's point of view:

> But I feel that if a writer had actually wanted a book to be read and so children were being asked to write a summary afterwards, they wouldn't have done it...there doesn't seem to be much purpose to it.

The teacher interviewing this boy clearly felt compelled to defend herself and all other English teachers of the personal growth model variety. She says rather plaintively:

> I feel I've got to put in the opinion of the English teacher here. I mean, I think the reason we do this is that what's supposed to happen is that we open your eyes a little bit. I mean, if it's fiction we end up talking about people and their behaviour. Hopefully that's what is really interesting. Hopefully.

A 16-year-old girl does suggest that reading a book in class can get you into a text that you might otherwise find difficult. This viewpoint is supported by a boy of the same age who describes his reaction to *Z for Zachariah*:

> I was sitting there, like this, just looking at the teacher but really falling asleep and I sort of started getting into it when strange things started happening.

An Inspector Calls is similarly discussed.

A 15-year-old girl balances her bite-size compliment with something more acerbic:

> I mean out of all the books I've been given (in school) I've never disliked any of them...But sometimes it's an awful lot of effort to get into it and I think, Oh why am I reading this book, it's rubbish.

Some of the more enthusiastic readers regard the set texts of the secondary school curriculum as an intrusion on their own private reading. One 15-year-old boy says this:

> The problem is, you get given a book and don't really feel like reading it anyway. And you're already reading a decent book that you picked and you want to read that. Then the teacher takes priority.

Another 16-year-old interviewee simply feels that there is no time for reading with all the school work to do. The need to study books to pass examinations is being completely ignored by another pupil:

> I don't think you should be forced onto books... I think if you don't want to read them you shouldn't have to.

CHANGES IN CHOICE

As already stated, all these comments were made at a time when teachers were relatively free to choose texts that matched their priorities. Teachers may have been glad of this freedom but pressure to be more prescriptive was mounting. At the very time when most of the interviews for the survey were being done, a Government body, The School Curriculum and Assessment Authority, was also finding out about literature in schools. A snapshot survey was conducted in March 1995 to find out what was being read by the pupils of 84 primary and secondary schools. One of its aims was to discover what was being studied in classrooms. When the report was published, most media reports dwelt on the failure of schools to teach the 'classics' at any stage of the school curriculum. Very few mentioned that the new orders for English, which were in operation by then, were bound to make significant changes to the literature taught in secondary schools. Now pupils' reading should include:

- two plays of Shakespeare;
- a drama by major playwrights (examples include Christopher Marlowe and R. B. Sheridan);
- two works of fiction of high quality by major writers published before 1900 (list supplied);
- two works of fiction of high quality by major writers with well-established critical reputations, whose works were published after 1900 (examples include James Joyce and Muriel Spark);
- poems of high quality by four major poets, whose works were

published before 1900 (list supplied);
* poems of high quality by four major poets with well-established critical reputations, whose works were published after 1900 (examples include T. S. Eliot and W. B. Yeats).

So if the snapshot survey conducted in March 1995 was an accurate reflection of departments' choices at the time, a similar survey done only a year later would almost certainly reveal a changed picture. An indication of how quickly the new orders are having an effect can be seen from analysing the texts bought by 22 South London English departments since January 1995. It is at Key Stage 3 rather than Key Stage 4 that there is a particularly marked shift towards introducing more 'classic literature'. Forty-seven sets of approximately 30 copies of pre-twentieth century texts had been purchased as opposed to only 25 sets of twentieth-century novels; Dickens' *The Christmas Carol* being the most popular purchase. The fact that many teachers have had to make changes to their choice of text in the light of the new English curriculum is not in doubt. The effect on pupils' perception of literature taught in the schools will be fascinating to follow.

STUDYING THE CHOICES

It is clear that it is not easy to choose books for study at any stage of the secondary school but perhaps it is the way that teachers present books to classes which makes the difference. Unlike primary schools, most pupils have a copy of chosen texts in front of them so the problem of following a story is reduced. However, despite the advice of many experts in the field of teaching literature, some teachers still seem to insist on reading round the class. An enthusiastic 13-year-old reader, asked why she finds school books so boring, replies:

Because when you have different people reading they always seem to read slower and it seems to take ages to read. I always go on ahead and have to come back after a few pages. They just seem to go so slow...

A 12-year-old pupil expresses similar frustrations:

Everyone reads at different speeds and if you take turns at reading a paragraph then some people read slow and if they stutter at words it doesn't sound the same. Everyone has different kinds of ways of reading books and one reads one way and then another person gets it and reads another way and it's really confusing. Whereas if the teacher reads it, how she reads it like Ms X really does act the part when she says the words which really is good.

Similar concerns are voiced by the Key Stage 4 pupils. One 14-year-old girl disliked *Macbeth* because most of the class read the words incorrectly and she was convinced that no one knew what was going on.

These comments should not go unheeded. Too many plots have been sacrificed for the sake of giving everyone a chance to 'practise their reading'. It's debatable whether it helps reading skills. As one girl of 12 complains, 'When I read out aloud I can't understand what I'm reading.' Certainly other pupils believe the practice is unhelpful:

I think it might be discouraging for the person who, if they are having trouble when they see the whole class, like, isn't finding it, like they are finding it boring and they might be really embarrassed.

Fox and Benton (1985), in their excellent book on teaching literature, claim that a teacher who cannot read aloud is 'seriously hampered'. They urge teachers to do the majority of reading of class texts so that teachers and pupils can share the power of stories. As they say:

There can be few more satisfying experiences for the teacher than those times when a whole class is 'hooked' on a novel. For once in a classroom, we know we are doing absolutely the right thing – sharing the spell of literature. The experience is almost physical, not only in the electricity of the attentiveness, but in postures and facial expressions.

In the interviews, teachers are praised for bringing texts alive. One girl enjoys her teacher's reading of *Boy* because 'Ms X has real expression'. If only more secondary pupils experienced books in the way that this girl remembers from her primary school:

I liked *The Secret World of Polly Flint* because ... we did that in Year 5 ... and it kept you on the edge all the time. And our teacher ... she'd get to a really good bit and then she'd close the book and we were all dying for some more.

Another 12 year old says:

I love it when Ms X reads. She puts on lots of funny voices for all the characters. It's much better when she reads.

READING BEYOND THE SET TEXT

Of course, the set text should be only one way in which secondary English teachers influence their pupils' reading. The notion of fostering independent reading has always been another aspect of their role. The National Curriculum, in both the new and old versions, certainly lays down that teachers should promote wider reading in order to develop independent, responsive and enthusiastic readers.

Of all the secondary pupils who filled in the questionnaire, only 3.7% felt that their teacher 'very often helped' them choose books while 45.6% said that they were 'never given any help' by the teacher. Surprisingly, there is only a minimal difference between the responses of the youngest and the oldest of this age range. Some of the other findings of the SCAA report discussed earlier support these responses. They found that children read less and less as they went up the school until, for 16 year olds, 'individual reading had almost entirely given way to the reading of set examination texts'. To some extent the blame for this state of affairs is pinned on the teachers who appeared to make very little attempt to promote their pupils' wider reading despite a National Curriculum requirement that individual reading must be monitored.

However there is evidence from the transcripts that teachers who attempt to encourage and discover new and exciting reading matter are recognised and appreciated by their pupils. One 12-year-old boy describes how his English teacher has been trying to encourage him to vary his reading and so he has been actively seeking different genres in his local library. Another boy in the same group interview develops the point by describing another approach of the same teacher.

> Ms X ... she's been telling us about books ... a couple of people in the class recommended some books and are lending them out and she said if you see a book you like that I've got that you would like to read then ask me if you can borrow it.

One girl felt sure that one way for teachers to encourage their pupils to read widely was for them to read carefully selected bits from books every week. Her teacher had started to do this and she had already been inspired to take home and read Berlie Doherty's *Street Child*; a book that she would not have chosen simply by looking at the cover or reading the blurb. Teachers who want to create a culture of reading in their classrooms and beyond can succeed but they need to realise that it is *their* responsibility to develop their knowledge of both the books available and the readers in their charge.

It seems harsh to suggest that secondary English teachers should do more when they are already under enormous pressure. Changes in the National Curriculum and GCSE examinations have already forced departments to reassess their approach to literature. However, the voices of these children suggest ways that teachers can help pupils to enjoy literature rather than endure it.

RECOMMENDATIONS

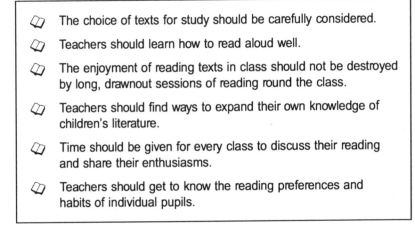

- The choice of texts for study should be carefully considered.

- Teachers should learn how to read aloud well.

- The enjoyment of reading texts in class should not be destroyed by long, drawnout sessions of reading round the class.

- Teachers should find ways to expand their own knowledge of children's literature.

- Time should be given for every class to discuss their reading and share their enthusiasms.

- Teachers should get to know the reading preferences and habits of individual pupils.

3

Home Reading

I just read a lot. I read a lot at bedtime. You see I'm kind of getting addicted to books. (*9-year-old girl*)

BEING READ TO AT HOME

The majority of interviewees could remember their parents reading to them at an early age, sharing books with them, telling them stories and rereading the same story. As Margaret Meek so clearly advocates, it is not just the aspect of being involved in the language of the book that is so important, but the need to let the narrative develop the young reader's imagination, along with giving them a sense of security and well being:

So the importance of reading stories aloud to children is not solely or simply to give them a rich experience of book language before they go to school. That will certainly happen. But the stories themselves provide the listeners with an increasing imaginative repertoire of ways of coming to terms with their emotions, which unlike all other aspects of their being, are full sized from the day of their birth.

On Being Literate (1991)

Books and stories make children feel good about themselves and their families. As this 12-year-old pupil clearly articulates, books were read to him in order to make him feel secure and comfort him:

Sometimes when I was lonely and needed cheering up, they'd come in and read a bedtime story. But since I've got older, when I was about three or something, they used to play story tapes.

The story, along with the presence of his parents, gave him the comfort to go to sleep. However, as he became older his parents assumed that a tape would compensate for their absence and that their child did not have the need for a 'live' performance – something which will be discussed later in the chapter. Reflecting on their own reading histories, older readers could also remember patterns, such as how they liked to be read the same book nightly. A 15-year-old boy reflects, 'I'd choose them, sometimes I'd have the same one every night.'

English for ages 5–16 argues quite clearly for this type of parental involvement.

> We hope parents will share books with their children from their earliest days, read aloud to them, and talk about the stories they have enjoyed together... Reading is best taught in the classroom when teachers build on this basis. (1989)

So significant were these practices that some readers could actually remember a particular title which was read to them nightly:

> I used to read *Quarrel in the Toy Shed* almost every night...Mum and Dad used to probably get fed up with reading it, but they let me read it anyway... it was just a habit anyway. (*15-year-old boy*)

This constant returning to a known and familiar text can signify that a child or listener is trying to work out something for themselves. They are coming to terms with their own emotions and have a need for security. We do not know what this young boy was working through, but the title would clearly indicate that the story was about an argument in a shed. If the boy had overheard, or witnessed, an argument which he could not understand, the story may have helped him to come to terms with the situation. However, looking back, as a 15-year-old, he justified this repetitive reading as 'just a habit', a throwaway line possibly to placate the interviewer, and to protect himself from more in-depth questioning:

Not all the interviewees followed the same pattern, that of returning to a favourite text again and again. Some liked to have new and fresh stories read to them nightly, to experience the thrill of a different narrative. As this 13-year-old girl states:

> I never wanted the same book, like in a short space of time, because I got bored with it if I'd heard it a short time ago. So I always wanted a different book every night. But I can't remember who chose it though. I think it must have been me.

Most readers interviewed did, however, remember having bedtime stories read to them by their parents and grandparents. Some were even carrying on the tradition by reading to their younger siblings. Through the discussions, 12-year-old readers were also able to reflect on what bedtime reading had given to them now, as readers:

> I used to get a bedtime story every night and I think that's really what gets you interested in books when you're older.

In contrast, some pupils could not remember being read to but in time had become avid readers.

As children mature and become more independent in their reading, parents often do not read them a bedtime story or hear them read regularly. Time may be a factor here, but just because an 8- or 10-year-old child can read it does not mean they will not enjoy cuddling up to a parent while sharing a common text. The sharing of a book will encourage parent and child to discuss the story, characters and plot. This then makes the reading a common experience, and brings the story to life for the younger reader. Reading aloud to children should not only occur when children are very young but should carry on at least until the end of primary education. Everybody likes being read to; it is that very pleasurable feeling of listening to a personal performance that will continue night after night, or day after day, as this 9-year-old girl describes:

> I haven't actually read *The Lord of the Rings*, but I've read *The Hobbit*. It's a thick book...and it was a very good book, very good. Very thick. We spend our entire holiday in France...when it gets to the hot weather, and you can do nothing but laze in the hammocks with...Mum would get out the book, and read to us. It was very good.

As Aidan Chambers (1991) states:

> Reading aloud to children is essential to helping them to become readers. And it is a mistake to suppose that reading aloud is only needed in the early stages (the period people tend to call 'learning to read'). In fact it has such value; learning to read is such a long-term process, and the bit we call 'learning' such a small part of it, that *reading aloud is necessary through the school years*.

THE IMPORTANCE OF TEXTS

Both the adults and the children who are involved in nightly sharing of books need to enjoy the story. Many books, such as *The Jolly Postman* by Janet and Allan Ahlberg, are multi-layered and give the adult, as well as the child, something to enjoy. If, however, the text is boring or repetitious then the reader will become bored and their reading of the text will reflect this, as described by this 14-year-old girl:

> [being read to by] Both of them. They took it in turns, or if I was lucky I'd get one off each of them...I think it's *Blackberry Farm*. My Dad used to skip out loads of pages because he hated them, they were so boring.

In contrast, this 15-year-old boy had memories of the actual pictures in the story books along with a fond memory of his 'nanny' reading to him:

> My nanny used to read me a bedtime story. It's more interesting with pictures, colour, bright, interesting.

It does seem, however, with an increasing range of taped stories that parents are replacing the bedtime story with a recorded version. With actors such as Alan Bennett reading *Wind in the Willows* and Martin Jarvis reading the *William* stories, parents cannot expect to compete on a similar level, but it is important that the tapes do not completely replace the live performance.

> Yes, Mum just used to put tapes on, so that she could go out and I was just listening to a story. Then she would come back in when it was finished, and turn the tape recorder off. (*12-year-old girl*)

At times mothers and fathers are busy and it is not convenient to read to the child, but it is important to share the experience, even of listening to the tape, together. An important aspect of reading is the response to the text, to predict what will happen next, to talk about the funny or scary bits, to talk about the style and to discuss the characters. If a parent watches a film or television programme with their child a discussion will often develop, and the same can easily occur when listening to a taped story. Reading is about sharing, whether it is a private reading or a performed text.

READING ALONE AT HOME

As well as being read to, children read privately in their homes. Initially this will be pretend reading for very young children, turning the pages and making up their own stories. From this stage of their reading development they then move onto becoming more independent. This 13-year-old boy has vivid memories of his private reading of *Paddington*, a book he has fond memories of and one with which he can identify as a significant stage in his personal reading history:

> I think when I was about eight I think. And I got given *Paddington* and it was six hundred and something pages. I think I got given it by my Nan and I always used to shout next door to my mum, like 'what's this word'. I always liked to shout and she could never get to sleep. I used to stay up for, like two hours reading the book because I was really interested in it. And after that book, I just couldn't stop reading. Like I couldn't go to sleep without reading.

Because the book was quite lengthy this young boy obviously developed stamina in reading and realised that he could read a book which was 'six hundred and something pages'; once this was achieved nothing would stop him reading, an obvious turning point in his reading career, and one that he still remembers.

Many of the pupils interviewed also mentioned that they read before they went to bed so that it would send them to sleep. But some primary age children also said that having computers, television or Walkmans in their rooms stopped them from reading. One girl felt that the computer was 'competing with reading', and these two 10-year-old boys preferred not to read:

> I don't read in my bed at bedtime, because I've got a television in my room, and so I just turn it on.
>
> I don't really read books at home because at night time I listen to my Walkman before I go to bed.

This 9-year-old girl articulates what the computer is doing in relation to the time she spends on private reading:

> Well...if I'd been nine, before I got the computer, I would have read a lot then...But now I've got the computer, it's also very...competing with reading. So really you have to decide, and spend an hour on the computer or sit down and read a book.

But this was not the pattern for all Key Stage 2 children. By contrast, some read at home instead of watching TV and often these were the children who liked to talk about where they read and why. As Aidan Chambers (1991) says:

And every reader knows that where we read affects how we read: with what pleasure and willingness and concentration. Reading in bed, feeling warm and comfortable and relaxed, is different from reading on a cold railway station waiting for a train.

The pupils who were avid readers read all over the house, in the bath, in their beds, on their beds, watching television and, in the case of this 10-year-old boy:

I've got this cupboard in my room which is really big, and I've got a light inside, and my sisters usually come in [to the room] and put the music on, so I sit in there [the cupboard]. I put the light on and read in there... I sit on teddies and things.

Having found a comfortable, secure, warm, quiet place in his bedroom this young reader was able then to lose himself in the reading matter. Other children mentioned that they read in various places in the house and at different times: 'in the bath... when I get home from school... in the night with my sister... just sit down on my bed'. They also read at home for different reasons '....whenever I get bored...to help me sleep.' Some children mentioned that they found it difficult to find a quiet place in the house to read, especially if they shared a bedroom with a sibling who listened to the radio or watched television on a regular basis. One Key Stage 2 boy in this situation read in the toilet, as it was quiet. However this boy said he did not like reading, although he had read *The Hobbit*. One wonders if the reason for his dislike of reading was that he could not find a quiet, comfortable place to read and thus become completely involved in the secondary world within the cover of a book?

INFLUENCES ON CHOICE OF BOOKS

Throughout the interviews it was demonstrated that the mothers of younger children influenced the children in what to read privately. Children talked about their mothers helping them choose books. Mothers would help in the choice of books while visiting the library, or going to the library for the children and actually giving them books they had read as a child. In the main survey 57.9% Key Stage 2 children said that their mothers sometimes, often and very often helped them when choosing books and this figure is consistent with the quotes from the interviews. Such an example is this 11-year-old boy:

I go to the library with my Mum, and she helps my brother and when I'm looking she gets books that she thinks I would like, and then she shows them to me.

A mother helping a child in this way is very beneficial, matching the children's reading needs to their interests, and guiding them to books that may appeal to them. This sort of guidance is invaluable, as it can open up different avenues of books for the young reader. An interested adult may be able to move a child on or direct a child to read a more varied diet of books. A child who is stuck on reading one author may, through this sort of guidance, be encouraged to read other authors who write in the same narrative genre or in a similar style. However, making a choice without the reader being present is always difficult, as this 10-year-old girl clearly outlines:

My Mum chooses me the books from Mansfield library because we don't get much time to go there, and she brings me quite good ones in. But she picks all long ones and you only get time to read about two or three. And books from the school library... I think it's a lot better than the Mansfield library.

Her mother's visits to the local library reflect the mother's obvious interest in her daughter's reading development. The books that are chosen are 'all long ones' which also suggest that the mother is choosing demanding texts. However, part of the developmental process of becoming a reader is the ability to be able to choose books for oneself, either from the cover and the blurb or, as one becomes a more experienced reader, from knowledge about the author or from recommendation. Thus, although this mother is helping her child by choosing books for her, she is not helping her to become a discerning reader, who can visit a bookshop or a library, browse the shelves and make an informed decision on what to read. We might also ask why the girl feels that the school library is better than the local public library. Is she judging the local library purely on the books her mother brings home? Would her opinion be changed if she were to visit the public library and choose the books for herself?

Other mothers of this younger age group of children strongly encouraged their children to visit the local library for homework and research, rather than for reading fiction. Of course this is an important aspect of reading, but it raises the question as to whether parents who rarely read fiction for pleasure and perhaps only read to find out information, have more pragmatic motives for reading and book selection:

That's what my Mum says. She says 'What have you got? Good heavens, why don't you go to the library and get some books because it helps you do your homework.' (*10-year-old girl*)

Thus we can see that from an early age mothers seem to give guidance as to the type of books and authors they would like their children to read. It is widely known that the ongoing popularity of the Enid Blyton books is due partly to parents recommending these to their offspring, because they themselves read them as children. Parents may even dig out their own collection of childhood books from the attic to give to their offspring. However, relying on childhood reading is limiting, as nowadays the range and variety of children's literature is vast and much would be missed. Unless parents are particularly knowledgeable or interested in the field of children's books they will only be able to recommend those books that they know about or have read themselves. The following four comments reflect some parents' recommendations:

My Mum said to me, *The Hobbit* might be something good for you, and she told me what it was about, and then I said 'Yes, I'll try this one', and then I got into it. (*11-year-old boy*)

...My Mum's book. My Mum said 'Why don't you try one of these?' (*12-year-old boy* asked why he reads *Biggles*)

Girl – Mum says I should read a bit more Charles Dickens, but...
Teacher – Do you?
Girl – No, not really. (*13-year-old girl*)

We've got quite a big collection of books at home... So I had a quick look at the bookshelves...They were there at home. And my Mum said yes, these were books I could read. She said have a go at one of these, and I liked it. (*13-year-old boy* talking about Agatha Christie books)

None of these books, suggested by the four mothers of these 11-, 12- and 13-year-old children, was written in the last 50 years. These mothers are not suggesting modern and relevant books to their children. The books fall into one of two categories, a classic or popular fiction. Both *The Hobbit* and Dickens can be regarded as classics as they have both stood the test of time and have universal values, as relevant today as when they were written. *Biggles* and Agatha Christie are both popular fiction, one written for children, the other for adults. Both are formulaic in approach and are part of a series; the mothers are relying totally on their own previous reading experience. By contrast, it is shown that adults recommending books can have a beneficial effect on a teenager's reading diet, as reflected in this discussion between two keen 15-year-old girl readers and their English teacher:

> *Teacher –* Have you read any Dickens?
> *Girls –* Yes.
> *Girl 2 –* *Great Expectations, Christmas Carol, Oliver Twist.*
> *Girl 1 –* Oh yes, I've read *Romeo and Juliet.*
> *Teacher –* Are you talking about things done in class?
> *Girl 1 –* I actually read it out of school.
> *Teacher –* For pleasure?
> *Girl 1 –* For pleasure, you know, to see what it was like.
> *Girl 2 –* I've read quite a lot of the classics because they were my Dad's and my Aunt's when they were younger and they've passed them on down to me and my brother. So I've read a lot of them, you know *Jane Eyre, Little Women.*
> *Girl 1 –* *Vanity Fair.*
> *Teacher –* You've read *Vanity Fair*? That's amazing because I haven't.

This interesting discussion reflects the range of personal reading that these two readers are covering in their own time, out of school. The material passed down reflects the reading diet of the father and aunt's own childhood, that of pre-twentieth century classics. Being avid readers, the girls are exploring the classics for themselves; however it is important for all readers to read a range of material. Peter Dickinson, in his essay in *Writers, Critics and Children* (1976) [edited by Geoff Fox *et al.*] argues that the material should be varied and should reflect the complete culture mix of the period, from the older classics, to modern books of literary merit and popular fiction.

As the pupils get older, their reading interest seems to converge with that of their parents. One 16-year-old girl talked of the link between her mother's reading and her own, that they read and enjoyed similar books and thus the choice was easier and common books could be shared. Also, parents who were still involved and interested with their offsprings' reading seemed to have reasonably clear ideas about the types of books that would interest them. This 16-year-old girl clearly has support from her mother and is beginning to choose more adult books with her help:

> *Girl –* Sometimes they'd give us books to take home from school and I didn't always like them so my Mum would find me something else she and I would like.

Teacher –   So your mum was a good judge of what you did like?
Girl – Yes.

The following 15-year-old boy, an avid reader, has the support and guidance of both his parents:

> My mum and dad know what I like because they see me reading all the time, so they'll get me that kind of thing. Or instead of giving me money to buy a book they'll take me into a bookshop and say, 'right, choose a book.' And then they'll buy it. And then if we're going away and there won't be anything to do in the evening or something we'll go out and buy a book each or something like that.

Reflected in this boy's description is a family that enjoys reading; the parents are in tune with their son's reading matter and encourage him by buying him new books. As he clearly states, they do not just give him the money, but take him to a bookshop to buy a book. One of the most enjoyable experiences for an avid reader is to browse in a bookshop and make a choice from the range available. And as Aidan Chambers (1991) states:

> Keen readers tend to be book buyers. We like to possess copies of the books that mean most to us. Owning them allows us to reread them when ever we want, helps us remember what is in them.

This particular family value reading for enjoyment. It is seen as something to do on holiday and at home for pleasure, and visiting a bookshop, as a family, is part of the pleasure of reading.

Some fathers do also play a part in guiding their children's reading. Sometimes this may be directed towards their son's interest in sport or sports personalities. An example of this type of engagement is given by this 11-year-old boy:

Teacher –   Where do you find books that you read?
Boy –   Well, for subjects such as rugby my Dad finds them for me, and I've got one at the minute called . . . it's an autobiography.
Teacher – He's a New Zealander, isn't it? Is it Nick?
Boy –   Yes. And I quite enjoy that. My Dad got it off a friend from work.

However, in the main survey it was found that at Key Stage 2 only 34.8% of fathers sometimes, often or very often helped their children choose books in comparison with 57.9% of mothers. Also within the survey it was shown that there was slightly more guidance given to boys by their fathers than girls by their fathers. For some boys, strong and careful guidance is needed as to what to read – guidance such as this father has given to his son which relates to a common interest. Some boys are reluctant readers and strategies are needed to lure them into being more independent readers, who gain pleasure from reading narrative. 'Boys are also less likely to read fiction for pleasure, but they do read a lot of football and computer game magazines.' (*Times Educational Supplement*, 6.10.95). By directing his son to read biography this father is encouraging his son to engage with the narrative form.

It does seem that a general pattern of reading emerges. Just as mothers and their teenage daughters begin to read similar reading material, some fathers may also suggest books for their children to read. What is interesting about the two following quotes is that both the books recommended by fathers have connections to television viewing. The programme or film may have been viewed together as a family, and having read the book the fathers then recommended them to their respective teenage children:

> I read one which was my Dad's book, and it was interesting, like the film called *The X-files* ... (*16-year-old girl*)

> With my Dad ... we watched a film, *The Eagle has Landed*, and he said there's a book about that, and I thought I'd read it. (*15-year-old boy*)

Older interviewees reflected, also, on their fathers' influence and guidance when they were younger.

> ... or my Dad used to bring me in tons of books or something ... he used to pick them out. (*12-year-old boy*)

> Yes, my Dad used to. ... he's a lorry driver and he takes a lot of books and toys and that to shops and he brought some of the books home. (*12-year-old girl*)

As mentioned previously, other members of the family also seem to be involved in suggesting books to the children, both in the primary age group and into secondary school. Often these newly experienced readers seemed to respect their grandmothers' opinion and enjoyed the recommended reading matter:

> And sometimes my Gran ... she's awfully good at crosswords, and she

often finds books in places and she saves them for me because she knows I enjoy reading. (*11-year-old boy*)

I went to my Gran's house and she's got the whole set. And she showed them to me and I said I'll try these. (*13-year-old girl* talking about James Herriot books)

Whether they were 10, 12 or 15 years of age, most of the children interviewed enjoyed the memory of being read to by their parents. Private reading at home, sharing books and talking about reading matter in general was considered to be an important part of their younger life. As they grew up, computers, television and videos competed with reading for time, but it did seem that if a young reader was into a book, or reading in general, they would find time to read, whether it was at bedtime or other times. The important message here seemed to be that the reading material needed to be of particular interest to the young reader, and family members need to tune into these interests and to be able to recommend suitable reading matter for them.

RECOMMENDATIONS

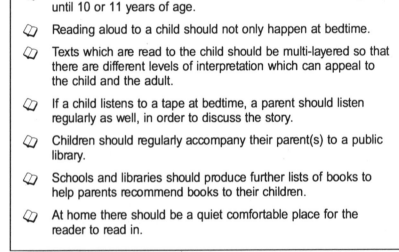

- Children need to be read to at bedtime from the earliest age, until 10 or 11 years of age.
- Reading aloud to a child should not only happen at bedtime.
- Texts which are read to the child should be multi-layered so that there are different levels of interpretation which can appeal to the child and the adult.
- If a child listens to a tape at bedtime, a parent should listen regularly as well, in order to discuss the story.
- Children should regularly accompany their parent(s) to a public library.
- Schools and libraries should produce further lists of books to help parents recommend books to their children.
- At home there should be a quiet comfortable place for the reader to read in.

4

Networking

Three 10-year-old girls are crowded round a three-sided swivel stand full of children's books in a local library. They are deciding which ones to take out for the week. Turning the stand, they spot favourite titles and talk animatedly about books and writers. For at least twenty minutes, they share views on good books they have read. The sight of Paula Danzinger's name sets them off on a swop of her best bits until one of them spies a new Betsy Byars' title and feels compelled to share her enthusiasm for it with the others. Impressed by the brief description, one of her friends decides to try it for herself. They continue to turn the stand until one takes out *Anne of Green Gables*. They all like the front cover but the length puts them off and so it is returned, unwanted. Suddenly one of them sees Malorie Blackman's *Hacker* and grabs it. 'Mine! Mine!' she shouts and the other two, realising what it is, try and prise it away. They all become rather desperate to claim the book for themselves. Anyone watching this small tussle would assume that it is over something far more valuable. Finally, the girl who first grabbed the book wins and she smugly agrees to let the others try it after her.

It is difficult to say why this book caused such passion. It had featured on *Jackanory* recently so maybe the influence of television can be thanked. But it is just as likely that it is the sort of book which gets read by one child and then knowledge of it spreads on the network of reading friends. These three girls will tell others about it and their enthusiasm will encourage new readers. This was certainly the case when Judy Blume's *Forever* was first published – it was read avidly because pupils talked about it while parents and teachers could do nothing to hinder or promote its popularity. *Hacker*, not having the slightly subversive element of *Forever*, may not become quite such a hit but this small scene is illuminating.

These primary school girls are a real example of pupils using their friends to decide what to read in much the same way as adults do. The results of the survey indicate that there are many other children at Key Stage 2 who value the influence of their friends. For all the primary school pupils who completed the questionnaire, 59% replied that their friends sometimes, often or very often helped them choose books. These figures remain steady throughout this Key Stage and can be compared with the responses given by the other people listed when this question was posed. Only mothers seem to be given similar credit, as was shown in the earlier chapter on home reading. However, far more revealing is the difference between the boys' and girls' responses. Girls credit their friends with influencing their choice of books much more readily than boys do. For example, 71% of 8-year-old girls ticked one of the positive columns for friends' influence in comparison with 45.9% of boys of the same age. For 11 year olds, it is a similar picture: 70.2% for girls compared to 48.8% of boys. The negative response is also interesting. For example, 54% of 7- and 8-year-old boys said that friends never or hardly ever influenced their book choice, while only 29% of girls felt the same.

The influence of friends on choice increases quite significantly for both sexes at the beginning of Key Stage 3. For many children, this is the start of their secondary school life. It is a time when parents disappear from the playground and the single form teacher is replaced by several specialist teachers. In the survey, 63.3% of 12 year olds said that friends influence their choice of book in some way while the percentage of children who claim that they receive little or no help from their peers drops to 36.8%. Again, the only other people with any significant influence on pupils of this age are mothers but they come a poor second, with 42% indicating that they turn to their mothers for some advice. There is still a sizeable gap between the responses of boys and girls. Seventy-eight per cent of girls aged 12 felt that their friends were important when it came to choice of books compared to 50.3% of boys.

These results appear at a time when concern about boys' achievement in English has become a national talking point. The fact that boys do less well than girls at GCSE English and beyond has been well documented for a long time but now there is evidence that the gap begins in primary schools. While some people are prepared to conclude that girls are simply better at English than boys, there are others who feel sure that it is the different cultures of boys and girls which make the difference. Girls are expected to like reading and no-one looks surprised if they sit around discussing books. The girls in the library scene seem quite natural but three boys behaving similarly might look out of place. Young boys are expected to share goal triumphs, not the latest Robyn Jarvis title. One way that matters might be improved as regards reading and boys could be if adults made positive steps to encourage book-talk among boys. The following interchange between two boys shows that sharing views on books can happen:

Teacher – Now, how did you choose that book? (*The Machine Gunners*)

Boy 1 – I didn't actually know it was what I wanted but then I came along to it and it looked quite interesting and I read the back and that sounded good. So I got really interested in it and I felt I had to read it.

Teacher – Good. And would you now go and read more books by Robert Westall, the writer?

Boy 1 – Yes because they've usually got the same sort of style.

Boy 2 – I've read *The Machine Gunners* as well but it had a different front cover. It sort of brought it more up to date. It doesn't have pictures in it, does it? In my – the one I read, it didn't have any pictures at all but something you might want to try – if you ever get to see it, is *Fathom Five*. That's another one – and it sort of carries on from *The Machine Gunners*.

Other interviews give further clues about how friends can influence the reading of both girls and boys. A 12-year-old girl who proudly describes herself as a bookworm then talks about how she discovers new books to read:

Girl – I find them in the library. We used to have a school library.

Teacher – Did the librarian tell you about good books or did you just find them on the shelves?

Girl – No not really. You just find them on the shelves unless you ask. If anything I ask my friends, like what books do they recommend or is this a good book if they've read it.

There are several other comments in a similar vein but friends' recommendations are not always the answer as this girl testifies:

I sometimes can't get into books – like it's a bit frustrating when you can't get into one. Let's say my friend has read something and I say, 'Is that a good book?' and she says, 'yes' and like I, well, I can't get into it.

Despite this remark, teachers should recognise how powerful a resource children's friends can be in the area of developing readers. As has already been suggested, boys will discuss their reading if they are given opportunities but all pupils can benefit from time in the school curriculum to talk about their reading with their peers. Instead of insisting on totally silent library lessons, part of the time can be allocated to sharing recommendations. Other possibilities are having a dedicated space on a display board for eye-catching book advertisements written by pupils or producing a regular news-sheet on best books read by class X.

A small classroom project gives an indication of how groups of pupils of both sexes can enjoy sharing books as part of their English work. The English teacher of a mixed ability class of 12-year-old pupils decided to replace the class reader slot of the first term with shared group reading. She chose six fairly recently published novels of varying difficulty. After an extensive period of 'selling' all the books, the pupils were given a fairly open choice, although the teacher managed to persuade individuals to pick the most suitable text for their ability. All groups were a mixture of boys and girls. Over five weeks, the groups read their separate books or worked on various written and oral tasks. The teacher became a roving supporter, helping the individual groups as she felt necessary. Towards the end of the project, each group was interviewed about the work they had been doing. Without exception, the groups were extremely positive. Only one girl felt that she would have preferred to have studied her book as part of the whole class. Over and over again, pupils talked of how much they enjoyed sharing their ideas in a group. Below are just a sample of their comments:

- It was good in a group because you got to really talk about the book. You can ask more questions.
- We got a better bond.
- I liked discussing the book with only a few people.
- It was nice to share ideas with your friends, with people at the same stage of reading.
- I liked reading a different book (from the other groups) because, well, you know reading something the other groups don't know and then you can say, 'look I really recommend this book.'

They also revealed that the project had encouraged them to lend books to others in their group. The four who studied Gillian Cross's *The Great Elephant Chase* wanted to read other books by her, so when one of them bought *On the Edge* at a school book fair the others asked to borrow it.

The survey also supports the view that borrowing books is popular among friends, particularly for secondary school girls. For 8-year-old pupils, only 16% of both girls and boys replied that they often borrowed books from friends. This figure hardly changes for boys but the percentage of girls who share books rises steadily as they grow older. For 15-year-old pupils, nearly 41% say that they often or very often use their friends' books as a source for their reading. As many of the pupils interviewed expressed concern at the price of books – 'They're too expensive and once you've read them, that's it' was how one girl put it. It is obvious that opportunities for borrowing through school lessons would be sensible.

It is not only the choice of books over which friends have some influence. The buying and sharing of comics and magazines can be analysed in relation to peer pressure. For primary school pupils, the survey and interviews revealed little acknowledgement of friends' influence. In the responses to the survey, the percentage of primary school boys and girls who borrow comics and magazines from friends never rises above 18% and the difference between the sexes is very little. Very few of the children interviewed attribute their tastes for comics or magazines to their friend. Instead they discuss their desire to find something that matches their interests. The following comment is typical:

> I've got a monthly magazine called *United*. It's about Man United. It's really good. It's got information in it and posters. It's really fun to read because they put jokes in it. (*11-year-old boy*)

Of course this boy's interest in Manchester United football team may be due entirely to wanting to support the best team around, even if it is miles away, but it is also highly likely that being a fan helps when making friends in the playground.

It is also important to note that the *Beano* was by far the most popular comic for this age group. In the survey, 526 respondents named it as their favourite comic; the next most popular title was the *Dandy* with 91 mentions. Undoubtedly humour is an important factor; the survey shows that funny stories are the preferred genre for this age group. But, in the same way that reading *United* must help when the talk is about football, sharing jokes about Gnasher is likely to cement friendships. So, although primary school pupils do not openly acknowledge their friends' influence, they do share similar reading matter.

There is less agreement about what is read in the secondary school. *Beano* and *Dandy* are still very popular but of the 13,514 respondents who revealed their favourite magazine, only *Just 17* had a sizeable amount of mentions (1709). Boys, in particular, do not have a shared interest in a single type of magazine. Their responses are spread over a wide range of subjects including computers, football, fishing. Girls, on the other hand, do tend to read 'teenage' magazines with 58% of them mentioning titles of this type.

Although there is a bigger spread of what is read by secondary school girls, they share comics and magazines more than do pupils in primary schools. The numbers increase immediately they are in the first year of secondary education and they continue to rise throughout the years. Of the girls of 16 who completed the survey, 41.5% said that they often or very often borrowed magazines from their friends. A comment from a girl of 15 may help to explain why this happens:

> You're more likely to find out that sort of thing (personal issues) in a magazine than books I think...from school or friends or whatever. You're more likely to just pick up a friend's magazine and find something in there, rather than actually going out and buying it.

More boys borrow magazines from their friends as they get older but the number never rises about 28%.

Peer pressure is often blamed for aspects of unacceptable social behaviour among the young. There is evidence from the survey and the interviews that, in the sphere of reading, we ought to welcome peer influence. As one 13-year-old girl said, 'I trust my friends' recommendations. They know what I will like.'

RECOMMENDATIONS

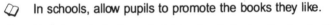

- In schools, allow pupils to promote the books they like.

- Help boys to feel comfortable about sharing the books that they enjoy.

- Find out about publications which include reviews of books by young people.

- Find space for group shared reading so that pupils can discuss the same book.

5

Gender Issues

Teacher –   Do you like reading?
Boy (15) –   No.
Teacher –   Do you think it is important?
Boy –   Yes.

This succinct exchange reflects the experience of many of those who are professionally concerned with developing the reading of young people and confirms much recent research evidence (Gorman, APU 1987/Gorman *et al.* NFER 1988, HMI 1993). Girls like to read, boys generally do not. Girls read fiction, boys stick to the sports pages of the newspapers. Girls explore their emotions through reading, while boys are more interested in exploring their hobbies. As they grow older boys maintain their interest in factual books but they may do so in an undifferentiated way. The survey showed that in the secondary phase girls make more selective use of reference books for course work and school related research, as they are more likely to use indices, appendices and to skim and otherwise to read selectively. To this extent, then, there was much evidence to support existing perceptions of gender differences and patterns of reading which are well known, almost taken as given. The danger is to assume that nothing can be done to alter what is almost a genetic disposition to reading and to become resigned and therefore reinforce the pattern. This is unfortunate because the survey and the interviews are susceptible to analysis and interpretations which suggest that some at least of these observed patterns are reinforced by attitudes and practices, in home and school, which tend to negate boys' sense of themselves as readers. Therefore the focus of this chapter is boys' reading, as it is seen to be problematic. Furthermore, as noted by OFSTED, while it has been the case that the underachievement of girls in Mathematics and Science has been the focus of much attention, that of boys in English has received far less attention until very recently.

Differences emerge early. In the infant phase boys are apparently more influenced by illustrations that girls, while girls are more inclined to base their choice on the title of a book. Hobbies and sporting interests emerged for the boys at Key Stage 2 as being a major factor in choosing books and magazines while girls read widely in a range of genres. Gender differences become more pronounced with age. In the primary phase, adventure, animal stories, horror and material related to hobbies are popular with both boy and girl readers. If anything, girls apparently read marginally more widely than boys. By the secondary stage it is noticeable that more girls than boys are enjoying diaries and romance, while sport, science fiction and hobbies remain favourite reading for boys. Girls talk to their friends and family about their reading. Younger boys will also do so, but by the time they are in their teens fewer than half will talk about books with friends, in the way discussed in the chapter on networking.

Of the younger children interviewed it was boys who were positively antipathetic to reading:

Teacher – Do you like reading?
Boy (9) vehemently – No, I hate it.

While there were girls who were less than enthusiastic about reading, it was rare to come across such blatant hostility. It is possible that this finding relates to the fact that boys' performance in reading lags behind that of girls. The APU surveys of 1983 and 1989 showed that differences noted at 11 years continued right through to GCSE stage. More recently, National Curriculum assessment is showing boys' scores to be consistently lower than those of girls in the key areas of reading and writing. Boys are more likely than girls to be placed in remedial reading groups and therefore to associate reading with a sense of failure and low self-esteem. This, however, offers only a partial account. If it is well known that boys' achievement in reading does not compare well with that of girls, remedial reading schemes may alleviate the problem in terms of raising reading achievement by a few months, but they do not answer the underlying question of *why* there is such a discrepancy in the first place. The OFSTED report (1993, page 27) noted the difficulties:

> The reasons for boys' poorer achievements in English are not identified easily. There is no firm evidence to suggest that the differences in boys' and girls' performance reflect differences in innate linguistic ability. Research studies on the existence of possible biological sex differences in language ability are inconclusive.

Increasingly the differences between boys and girls are being discussed in terms of social and psychological factors. One small-scale study (Pugh

1995) highlights the notion that boys feel insecure in the affective areas of English because, unlike Science and Mathematics, there are no clear facts to be assimilated. One of her respondents said 'When you read a book, it's like delving into people's lives. It's being nosy.' This point of view is a general one among the boys in the survey.

There is a strong sense of resistance to certain reading *practices* as well as the more widely recognised one of *genres*. The National Curriculum does not sanction the kinds of reading typically favoured by boys. At the same time it demands approaches to books with which boys are uncomfortable. This includes the analysis and the exploration of ideas in discussion and writing that is the focus of much school-based reading. Among the older boys, there was resentment at having to reread books. Interestingly, however, they were quite keen to reread books they had enjoyed at a much younger age; some of them referred with nostalgia to the *Postman Pat* series and to unlikely sounding titles such as *Quarrel in the Toy Shed* and *Five Little Kittens*. Some older boys who were not enthusiastic about reading themselves said that they liked reading 'babyish' books to younger brothers and sisters, possibly because it gave them a context for reading in which they felt both confident and competent. What they do not like is the reflective rereading analysis that is required for English at secondary level.

> *Boy (15)* – I don't think you should be forced onto books... if you don't want to read them you shouldn't have to.
> *Teacher* – What about what I do with you then?
> *Boy* – Well that's different, but I feel that if a writer had actually wanted a book to be read so children were being asked to write a summary on it afterwards they wouldn't have done... there doesn't seem to be much purpose to it.

As suggested in Chapter 2, the boy allies himself with the author here, but more than this he questions the whole approach he is being asked to take when he studies texts in class. This attitude was very prevalent among boys. Another 16 year old was even more explicit:

> I like to read, but I don't like to read like an English teacher. People are totally put off by having to look at this and having to look at that. You should read to relax....

Again the message is plain. It is not reading as such that deters boys, but the process of analysis and reflection that goes with it. Another practice widely disliked is that of keeping up a reading log or diary. It is one thing to make a simple list of books read, but as one 12-year-old boy explained:

> It's nearly stopped me reading books. Every time I finish one my teacher makes me write a review of it, so that makes me feel like not reading so much because I don't like having to do that.

It does not, however, follow from this that boys are not interested in reading about feelings as such. Apparently they simply do not like having to analyse them afterwards. Any teacher who has carried out classroom work on comics and magazines will know well that, while girls are not avid readers of *Improve Your Coarse Fishing*, or many of the other titles likely to be supplied by boys, the problem pages of *Just Seventeen* or the 'how to do it' articles in *Sugar* are avidly read by both sexes. The boy who said 'I read the problem pages of *Just Seventeen*... it's a good laugh' is typical and is probably looking for more than just a 'laugh'. Many boys turn to the pages of publications nominally targeted at girls in order to find out answers to their dilemmas about growing up. It is perhaps interesting to note that while publications aimed at adult males, such as *GQ* and *Esquire*, set out to address the 'new man' at least occasionally, through articles which aim to confront stereotyping and to consider issues of men's health, there is as yet no publication for the 'new boy' that considers his problems with relationships, adolescence and acne, in the same way. Unsurprisingly, then, boys look to the pages of the magazines intended for girls for answers to problems that worry them deeply. Phillips (1993) quotes one 15-year-old boy:

> One of the main things I worry about is masturbation. I've tried a few times but nothing has happened. I've read all about it in books and magazines and heard what it's like from friends. They say that they do it every night and that it's really good. I think I'm going through puberty too slowly, or something's wrong.

What is interesting about this is the fact that while he is able to talk about sexual matters with friends it is not particularly helpful as, in the main, they are keen to boast about their own experiences. Nor have the books and magazines he has read answered his emotional needs or explained away his anxiety. He is not alone in this. In the survey only half of the boys felt that reading about such matters was helpful while two-thirds of girls thought it *was* useful.

This may be because boys tend to choose factual material and to be selective in what they think is relevant to them. Some of the sharpest differences shown up by the survey were related to experiences of reading about sex and health problems. While 80% of girls had read about pregnancy, fewer than one-third of the boys claimed to have done so. Why not? 'Because I am a BOY!' said one, as though it were self-evident that it was of no relevance to him at all. Girls were far more likely to have read about contraception and abortion than boys, although interest in AIDS was shared. Boys were more likely to have read about homosexuality. Overall, while both sexes read about a wide range of topics related to health and sexual matters, two-thirds of boys said they preferred to rely more on factual material for answers to their questions while girls were much more likely to identify with fictitious accounts. More than one, for example, mentioned *Forever* by Judy Blume, with its explicit description of a first sexual encounter. It may explain the fact that girls, who had read more contextualised and complex accounts, were twice as likely to feel that reading helped them with their understanding of growing up than were the boys.

It follows from this that boys may be constrained in their reading habits by two factors: firstly, availability of material that meets their needs and secondly, their sense of what is seen as being appropriate and relevant to them. There is powerful evidence that boys' reading habits are shaped strongly by peer pressure. This pressure can be exerted equally by both girls and boys. This is shown clearly in the following exchange between 15 year olds:

> *Girl 1 –* I read non-fiction for course work, but I wouldn't pick it up and say 'that looks interesting'.
> *Boy –* I might read car books, but I don't really read much though (*all laugh*).
> *Girl 1 –* You could look at the pictures though.
> *Girl 2 –* It's more boys, isn't it, that look at non-fiction.

There seems to be a general acceptance here that reading is something that boys do only reluctantly, and if at all then only in certain areas. Boys' reading is a bit of a joke. In another interview a 16-year-old girl reacts scornfully to her teacher's suggestion that she might read Terry Pratchett:

> *Girl –* No, I don't like him, I think he's stupid.
> *Teacher –* Is Terry Pratchett a very male writer?
> *Girl –* Yes, well because all of the boys in our year, well most of them, they've all read them haven't they?

At one stroke she has neatly defined the reading interests of most of the boys in her year group as well as disparaging a taste she plainly regards as being juvenile. There was little evidence in any of the interviews of boys and girls discussing their reading with one another and when it does occur it tends to be negative, as in the previous exchange. Taken to extremes it appears that in mixed schools girls sometimes sanction what boys may read. Two 12 year olds who happened to be good friends and who did talk about books together provides a fascinating glimpse of this in action. This is what Gemma has to say:

> Some of the books that I read aren't suitable for boys...like Judy Blume has got one called *Are You There God? It's Me Margaret*, and Paul picked it up at the library when we went down there together and I said 'No you can't read that I'm sorry'. And then he read the back and he said 'I see what you mean'.

The consequence of this is that Paul learns his lesson. He has this to say:

> Sometimes you really want to read a book but you have to read it at home because if you took it into school someone would laugh at you for reading it.

Paul then takes up solitary reading at home because he is concerned that he might be ridiculed for his choice of books, or at least he is careful to read in public books that will be non-controversial choices. This explicit account of a girl defining what her classmate may read is possibly unusual, but in more insidious ways there is considerable evidence of a similar pressure affecting boys' reading choices. The strand of thinking was discernible in several schools. Here is another 12-year-old boy talking about his pleasure in reading *Little Women*, which he was reading at home. Firstly, he describes his impression of the book:

> It's such a nice sweet story. I can really picture it in my mind brilliantly...I like Jo, she's funny and bouncy and full of life.

Clearly he identified, in a very unselfconcious way, with the character with whom most girl readers associate themselves, while the psychological reality of family life in the story appealed to him directly. But he and his friend (also aged 12) are aware that there are social consequences in being seen to be enjoying such a story:

> *Boy 1* – I don't really hold with all of that rubbish, boys' books and girls' books. If a boy enjoys a book then I don't think that anything

should come between him and that book.

Teacher – What might do that?

Boy 2 – Well some people are sensitive about comments. It mostly applies to boys. If a girl reads a boys' book that's not too bad. But if a boy reads a girls' book then it's a whole different story.

Teacher – Who would say anything?

Boy 1 – Well if Andy or I came in with *Little Women*, then I just know that people in the class would take the mickey... mostly boys who don't really read themselves so they don't really appreciate books and they don't understand....

Boy 2 – ...and the girls who don't like reading would be the same: 'Oh, look at him, he's reading a girls' book....'

Boy 1 – If it was me I wouldn't really care but I think some people would be bothered.

This differs profoundly from attitudes expressed by the girls. Sometimes they have strong views on the apparent intention of a book: 'I don't like the cover of *The Machine Gunners*... it makes it seem just a boys' book...' (*12-year-old girl*) But not one of them suggests that she would be laughed at or subjected to social pressure for choosing a particular book, or being seen to read a book ostensibly intended for boy readers. If girls reject a book then they tend to do so for reasons of personal preference rather than because they feel pressured by the need to maintain appearances.

It does, however, seem to be possible to overcome some of the inhibitions on boys' reading, whether self-imposed or perceived from others. As noted by HMI (1993), though rarely encountered it is the case that in some schools where reading is actively promoted for all, it is possible to create a culture of shared interest in books that will involve boys and girls. One group of 12 year olds in the survey talked at length about their preferences in private reading and about the books they had enjoyed in class. The boys in this mixed class were deliberately grouped together to talk about their reading and preferences. From this they began to develop an understanding of each other's tastes and in the class there was plenty of evidence of boys recommending books to each other, and of sustained reading and discussion of books in class and outside, with library visits and exchange of books brought from home. A further significant factor was that the class teacher was both knowledgeable about children's literature and open minded about the books that boys would enjoy. She felt that boys' reading needed to be encouraged because they sometimes seemed less aware of the range available to them. One of the boys in her class had this to say:

My teacher has been saying you should vary what you read, like read a bit of poetry, try a bit of mystery, so I went to the library and I did, and then I read *Blubber* and from there I've read lots of different books.

There is plenty of evidence from this and other similar observations that it is indeed possible for teachers to influence the range of reading undertaken by boys and girls. In order to do so they need to have an initial understanding of the preferences and reading skills of the pupils in the group in respect of private reading. Additionally they need to have a good knowledge and understanding of the available literature. While primary teachers may have this, the impression of the survey was that this is a relatively rare attribute of teachers at the secondary stage. This may be unfair in the sense that the interviews focused on the pupils' account of their reading rather than that of the teacher. However it was noticeable that the range of books recommended by teachers tended to fall within a fairly well-established 'unofficial' secondary reading curriculum, underpinned by the reading requirements of the GCSE.

The perception of the teacher referred to was supported by comments made by other boys in the interviews. While girls seemed to be clear about their likes and dislikes, boys sometimes appeared to be aimless in their choices. One of the conclusions of the pilot for the main survey was that 'boys are prepared to make independent choices earlier than girls' (Reynolds 1994). The basis for this was the fact that boys were much less inclined than girls to indicate that adults, be they teachers, librarians, parents or friends, had influenced their choice of books. The main study and the evidence of the interviews suggest that independence may not necessarily be a positive attribute. While some boys make confident choices, many operate in a vacuum, slightly confused and reading almost at random:

The lady over the road, she done a book sale... (*15-year-old boy*)

Well if the book's there and even if it looks boring you might eventually pick it up because you had nothing else to do. (*16-year-old boy*)

Well usually I just go by the cover. (*15-year-old boy*)

The fact that they do not readily turn to adults for advice should not be taken as evidence that boys are able to make good choices for themselves. Very often these fairly random choices made on a superficial basis prove to be disappointing reads and are left unfinished. One boy disliked being guided in ways that he felt were the expected patterns:

When I ask in the library, they always say why don't you try the science
fiction. Lots of my friends like those kinds of books but I don't really.
So it's sometimes a bit difficult to find something I like (*14-year-old boy*)

His teacher set out to help him by deliberately choosing genres and authors
that he had not yet encountered including biography and journalistic
writing (she mentioned Tom Sharpe) as well as fiction.

A children's librarian keen to promote boys' reading made a similar
observation, suggesting that biography, with its combination of personality,
factual detail and strong narrative drive, was an area of boys' reading which
might well be encouraged. The evidence of the survey data is that as a genre
it is favoured by girls, possibly those who reject factual writing on the whole
and therefore teachers may find it valuable middle ground in some groups.
Other factors she identified were to do with publishing conventions. Less
able boys were often daunted by typography, by dense page layout or by the
appearance of the jacket. It has already been noted that boys are more
influenced by cover design than tends to be the case for girls. In her
experience it was the case that boys are often put off a book which might be
of interest because of a jacket design that featured a girl or one that looked
depressing. This certainly seems to be an issue for some boys. One 12-year-
old boy who had been recommended *Kezzie* by Teresa Breslin was adamant
that he would not read it because the cover portrayed a girl and this made it
seem very much a 'girls' book' to him, in spite of the assurances of his
teacher that he would enjoy it.

Another issue the librarian identified was boys' unwillingness to engage
with the real world, or at least the view of it presented by many currently
rated authors writing for teenagers. Their dystopian world view, focusing
on pollution, family trauma and social breakdown, is one with which many
boys feel ill at ease. Many choose humour, escapism and fantasy. They
gravitate to Christopher Pike and James Herbert partly because the themes
are safe, dealing with situations which are not likely to happen to them
personally. A related genre which is known to attract many boys, and
possibly for just these reasons, is the graphic novel, combining as it does the
interplay of text and graphics, with the subversive appeal of fantasy and of
the comic book. Only one boy referred to these 'comics' in the interviews,
apparently in the belief that his teacher would not be interested in such
reading matter. This underlines the fact that many boys apparently find
their preferences in reading are not validated by the curriculum or condoned
by teachers or parents. One outcome of this is that an interesting aspect of
boys' reading may have been overlooked: when collating all of the references
to books made by boys and girls, the boys were reading a wider range of

material: girls confining themselves almost exclusively to fiction while boys ranged into other genres. This raises the issue that although many existing ideas about gender differences are confirmed by this study, there are complexities discussed here which teachers, librarians or parents may explore further and while finding out more about the reading habits of boys, they may do much to encourage their development as independent readers.

RECOMMENDATIONS

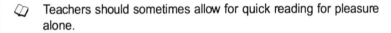 Teachers should sometimes allow for quick reading for pleasure alone.

Single sex reading groups may be helpful in encouraging boys to talk about their reading.

It helps to introduce boys to different genres and styles of writing.

Teachers and parents should find out what boys are reading.

It is useful to develop critical awareness of packaging and presentation of books by talking about these issues.

6

Access to Books

A typical primary school, suburbia: 1950s

The books are in ordered piles: *Janet and John, Nip and Fluff*, graded reading schemes, used in the same session of 'reading practice' each day, places marked with a card recording progress. Once you have completed the whole series, you may, and this is a special privilege, be promoted to the top readers' group and be allowed to progress and to choose from the special shelf which contains the prized copies of Enid Blyton, Richmal Crompton and Arthur Ransome. The editions are plain, cloth covered, close printed with line drawings, the paper is cheap utility. The books do not feel good to handle, but even with this restricted access they are often dog-eared and shabby.

Same school: 1990s
Baskets and racks of books, colour coded so that young readers may choose books within their ability range, on the topic table well illustrated reference books, a book corner with shelves packed with attractively produced and illustrated picture books, legends, stories, novels. Down the corridor is the library area with floor cushions and comfortable seating, books for all topics covered in the curriculum. In the corner, the television, the computer.

There should be, then, no problem. It is evident that most children, even those in relatively deprived circumstances, have far greater access to a wider range of attractively produced books than ever before. In 1993 there were over 7000 books published for children in Great Britain. Children's publishing as a sector of the industry is expanding rapidly: between 1985 and 1990 children's book sales increased by 170% while adult book sales increased only 47% over the same period. While in 1966 the Plowden report revealed that as many as 29% of homes had fewer than five books in them, 30 years on the vast majority of the children involved in the current survey had ready access to books. The question of access to books, then, needs to be qualified. In spite of all of the changes for the better in provision of books, what is remarkable is that some children in the survey expressed an inability to find material they wanted to read, and plenty more simply do not read. If there is an access problem then there needs to be consideration of how young readers can make sense of the immense range available to them; and what that range may be at different stages of their development. It needs consideration of the roles of different adults professionally involved in guiding choice and a look at resource issues generally and how they may affect particular groups of children.

The survey set out to find out about the sources where young people find their books and other reading material.

Source	Percentage of 11–16 year olds borrowing books quite often or more frequently (%)
Public library	68
School library	65
Friends	56
Parents	41
Classroom library	25
Brother/sister	22

Family relationships and attitudes to books and reading are dealt with elsewhere. Here the emphasis is on formal access to books through public libraries and schools.

PUBLIC LIBRARIES

The public library is the most popular choice for borrowing books across the whole of the age range in the survey and use of the library remains remarkably consistent, with 66% of the 4–7 year old age group borrowing books often. Clearly patterns of use vary. In the early stages many of the children talk about visits with parents:

Does the librarian help you? Or is it just your mum?
Just my mum.
Do you ever ask the librarian for any help?
No. I just look at the...my mum does sometimes. I usually use the computer there.
Oh do you? Good! And how do you look up the books then? Do you look at shelf numbers?
No, I've just got onto *The Hobbit* and the *Biggles* books. I used to type

Biggles or something and it had the whole list of them. All the *Biggles*
books. And you could see if they're in. (*10-year-old boy*)

This young reader is learning how to pursue his preferences and to make
sense of the library alongside a parent. The discussions also revealed the
constraints on access to books through libraries:

Well I used to use the library a lot. I used to go there about once a week,
but then I kept forgetting to take my books back and Dad always had to
pay the fines, so he banned me. I think libraries are really good. They've
got a really good selection of books.

This seemingly trivial, if sad, exchange illustrates the ways in which pressure
on family budgets as well as constraints on public expenditure can restrict
access to books at important stages. It is not too much to ask, perhaps, that
younger readers should not automatically be made to pay fines on overdue
books, as is already the case in some authorities. Other aspects of
frustration with the public library emerged. In some areas of the country,
branch libraries are being closed due to cuts in public spending. Some
children in the survey found themselves a bus-ride away from their nearest
library or dependent on visits from the mobile library. Opening hours were a
problem for some and others, who could use the catalogue, found other
aspects of locating books a problem:

There's no system of finding out whether anyone's got it... I mean the
books in the library...but there's no way of telling if it's there or if
someone else has got it....

If the key to becoming a keen reader is having access to the right book at the
right time (possibly a truism, but see Hunt, 1993 for a detailed discussion of
this), then the public library has a key role to play. Here is an 11 year old
talking about how she became hooked on reading:

I think I saw a book review on television and I liked the sound of the
book so I got the book out of the library and I liked it and I just started
from that.

Libraries and librarians work hard at encouraging young readers. The
Library and Information Statistics unit at Loughborough University report
that 90% of authorities hold regular storytelling sessions, 73% have year-
round events, three-quarters provide books and materials in minority

languages, school holiday events are held in 90% and reading schemes in 68%. All of this is encouraging. It is worth reflecting, however, that these and many other initiatives such as class library visits are aimed at younger readers. It is unusual for organised schemes for involvement with the public library to involve readers of secondary school age or those making the transition from the junior to the adult section of the library. Some are quite clearly put off by what seems a daunting step:

> I didn't know you could just borrow any book. I thought you had to get books...there's a 'teen reading section', and I thought you had to get the books from there until you got a special ticket. (*11-year-old girl*)

In the survey as a whole, very few children claimed to be helped in their choice of books by a local librarian. When a relationship does emerge it can be a powerful one. A graduate about to embark on her postgraduate teaching course explained that her love of literature derived from her relationship with the children's librarian she had know since infant school days, who had come to know her and her reading preferences and was always able to suggest the book that met her needs of the moment all the way through school and into university. This relationship is special and rare and implies a degree of continuity and expertise which cannot always be guaranteed. The very large majority, 80% of 11 year olds for example, never or only rarely get help from the librarian in making their choice, although there is some evidence that children perceive the staff of the junior library as being more supportive and approachable than those in the adult lending section.

This may be because a large proportion of young readers are confident and competent users of the public library and more willing to browse there than in the school library. Older readers often talk about using the jacket blurb, actively looking for books that appeal:

> I went to the library and I went through to the horrors and I saw the front cover and thought that looks quite good and I read the back of it about the description and I enjoyed reading that and so I thought 'Why not?'. (*11-year-old boy*)

It is noticeable, however, that very few readers think to enlist the help of the librarian in choosing books, particularly fiction. They are far more likely to be guided in their choices by friends and personal preference. Experienced and confident readers will take risks and venture into areas they have not tried before, because they have a more strongly developed sense of what will appeal. Some become sophisticated users of the library; two keen 15 year olds said they regularly ordered books from the library on the basis of reviews they had read in magazines, but they are not typical. Many others will have given up the fiction habit by this age or resort mainly to series books which are 'safe' because they are familiar in format and style. A possibly negative aspect of this is that libraries may respond by stacking the shelves with the current favourites, *Goosebumps* or *Sweet Valley High* rather than a wider range of authors and genres.

THE SCHOOL LIBRARY

Attitudes to the school library shifted across the age ranges surveyed. Younger pupils were more likely to find the school library a principal source of books for reading for pleasure. One girl in junior school describes how she felt when she realised she had only one year to go before moving on to secondary:

> I started really reading books when I was in Year 5 because there was such a big library here I felt I had to read all the books before I got onto another library...well all the fiction ones anyway (*dissolves into giggles*).

This enthusiasm for the school library as a source of books for reading for pleasure diminishes with age. The evidence of the interviews shows that while friends are a prime source of books to be read for pleasure, by the secondary phase the school library is associated primarily with material linked to the curriculum and course work:

> I go down to the library sometimes...I get books because we need them for a project or something....
> Yes, like me and my friend last year, we did about Explorers as a topic and we needed loads of books....
> And then we're doing another one this year, about the Romans...and it's really hard to find loads of books about it.

These Year 7 pupils illustrate their utilitarian attitude to the library. They use the school library for specific purposes linked to class work and they expect to find suitable material. It is also plain that they are becoming more demanding in their expectations of library provision. While their counterparts in the 1950s might have been satisfied with a single encyclopaedia reference to the Romans, these children want to find 'loads of books'. This may derive from a 'more is better' mentality but it is at least as likely that it results from shifts in the curriculum and approaches to study. The emphasis now is no longer on simply finding information but on evaluating evidence, balancing different views on a topic and examining different approaches. In these terms this boy's demand for several books is a legitimate one. It may then be perfectly reasonable to suggest that while provision of books has increased, that there are circumstances in the late twentieth century which indicate that alongside advances in Information Technology, young readers need enhanced access to books, which many of them feel they do not receive. Another 12-year-old girl said 'I think the library should have a wider range... more fiction... more fiction for children... '. A boy of the same age said:

> There's not that good a range really, most of the books they have are for work, like History and Geography. The story books they have don't really interest me, they look old and dusty... and then when they get new ones in, well it's first dibs really, they all go pretty quick.

One reason for the perceived gap, may be the difficulty that the schools library service is experiencing in meeting the demands made upon it. There is clear evidence that the perceptions of these young readers about the shortcomings of the school library are real. School library services are not statutory and are therefore vulnerable to cost-cutting. The Library and Information Statistics Unit report that in 1994–5, fewer than 14% of local authorities spent at recommended levels on school library services (the formula being that spending should reflect the percentage of children in the population). It is at least possible that current trends will widen the gap in provision between relatively affluent and deprived areas: Gloucestershire and Berkshire, for example, spend more than twice the recommended amount while Newcastle, the Rhondda and Hammersmith and Fulham all fund school library services at well below the level which might appear to be reasonable.

If this is true at Authority level then the differences are even more evident at individual school level. In 1995, according to the Educational Publishers Council, one of the highest spending primary schools was an independent school in Hampstead where the expenditure on books was £80 per pupil. Nearby in Ealing a local authority school had only £33 per head for all consumables and reckoned to spend less than £3 per head on books, with nothing at all spent on the library. The gap in provision for pupils from relatively affluent homes and those from more deprived backgrounds is emphasised by the suggestion from a teacher in the former school that the parents were likely to spend at least £80 each on books for use at home, a figure unlikely to be equalled by the parents of the children in the Ealing school. The general decline appears to be increasing: overall English counties are set to spend 14% less on school library services in the coming year than they did four years ago. The consequences of this in a period of rapid curriculum change are serious. As noted earlier, two-thirds of young readers borrow books from the school library often or very often. The downside is that an average of a one-third of all teenagers never or hardly ever borrow a book from the school library. By Year 11 the figure is well over half, with 56% of the age group never or hardly ever borrowing a book from the school library. The reasons for this may be complex: they may reflect the move away from course work for example, although most GCSE subjects continue to demand a degree of independent research. It may be that pupils will use the library for reference purposes rather than for the sustained reading which involves borrowing books. However, some evidence of the interviews suggests that the school library falls between two stools: on the one hand very keen and experienced readers find the choice in the school library limiting. Here are two very able readers, 15-year-old girls talking about their library use:

> I use the town library a lot, but the school library I hardly ever use... I mean if I'm doing a project, I usually get my books from there because the school libraries don't always have the same choice....

> ...yes, I use the school library about once every two months or something like that, not very often at all....

> ....I tend to go to the town library for reading books, but I might go to the school library if I'm doing a project or something.

On the other hand, less committed readers are progressively less likely to borrow from the school library because they are unaware of what it has to offer and lack the confidence to find out.

However this does not mean necessarily that they never use the library. In fact, they may do so for a whole range of purposes which do not involve books. A significant factor in patterns of library use is the widening of the scope of the service, to include Information Technology, a fact which is reflected in the redesignation of the library in many secondary schools as a Learning Resources Centre. Many pupils will choose the CD Rom rather than a book. One of the reasons cited is that for some, at least, it is more easily accessible:

Our teacher told us not to take books out of the library because there wouldn't be enough if we all went to look. So I looked on the CD Rom, because when you go to look for the book sometimes it's not there or someone else has got it. The CD Rom is simpler. All you have to do is to click a button. (*13-year-old boy*)

The consequences of this are interesting. An unquestioning enthusiasm for new technology combined with a shortage of relevant printed matter may result in uncritical literacy. Currently politicians of all parties are keen to advocate wider access to Information Technology, including the notion that all schools should be connected to the Internet. This view may need to be questioned critically. Anecdote already shows concern from some teachers about projects consisting of chunks of the *Encarta* or *Grolier* encyclopaedias, downloaded and pasted up attractively.

A surprising finding was that the readers surveyed did not regularly enlist the help of the school librarian in helping them to choose books. The figures remain surprisingly consistent. Primary schools do not have librarians as such, so the question was not asked of them. But even in the secondary age range more than 70% of the 11 year olds surveyed, rising to 82% of the 16 year olds, said that they rarely or never had help from the school librarian in choosing books. This is a figure which is disconcerting. Taken positively it may reflect a healthy independence. In one of the most consistent of all of the survey responses 90% of all those surveyed claimed to choose books by themselves. This needs to be set against the fact that by the end of formal education at 16, 45% of teenagers say they never or only rarely read fiction for pleasure. This suggests that there may be a need for greater mediation of the contact between reader and book. There could, for instance, be a shift in the emphasis in library lessons which tend to focus on the systems of cataloguing and the arrangement of the library, to include more sessions on genres, authors and the range of the material available in the library. It may also mean that school librarians need to emphasise the aspects of their role and expertise which are to do with helping individuals in a general way in their choices, particularly in fiction, as well as helping them find, for example, the right book for a History project.

BUYING BOOKS

When it comes to acquiring books to keep, a range of sources emerged (including the books mentioned in Chapter 3 that literally came off the back of a lorry). More conventionally the main survey showed that buying books was a relatively popular activity. These are the figures for the 11 to 16 year old who may be assumed to be making independent choices about buying books:

Source of books	Used often or very often (%)
Bookshop	72
Newsagents	25
Book club/mail	16
Book fair	11.5
Supermarkets	7.5
School bookshop	7.0
Jumbles/charity shops	7.0

Again, analysis shows that there are considerable discrepancies between different age groups. Buying from bookshops remains consistent across the age group while buying books from charity shops, jumble sales or the newsagents becomes marginally more popular with the older readers. All the other categories fall off markedly. The diminishing interest in supermarket purchasing possibly reflects the fact that older children are less likely to accompany parents on shopping trips. It also relates to the range of books stocked in those outlets. Sainsbury's, for instance, carries a range of books intended for beginner readers and also blockbuster fiction in its foyer vending areas, but there is nothing of specific appeal to teenage readers. The situation may be about to change markedly, however, with the abolition of the net book agreement. Asda supermarkets reported £100,000 of increased sales on books over a three-month period in late 1995 which they attributed to new business rather than a shift from more established outlets. This may be the beginning of a new trend which will affect teenage buying habits.

Buying books from sources in school such as clubs run by teachers, school bookshops and book fairs and exhibitions such as those sometimes run in Children's Book Week seem to appeal far more to younger readers. For example, while 47% of 11 year olds would buy from a book fair, only 16% of the 16 year olds were attracted. School bookshops seem to be in decline relative to ordering schemes, possibly because of constraints on teachers' time. It may be the case that ordering from schemes such as the Red House Club is a familiar activity and a habit which persists from junior school into the lower years of the secondary phase. It is noticeable too that their appeal may rest on the fact that many of the titles offered are TV and film tie-ins or have some other novelty value. Fewer than 2% of 16 year olds used them often as a source of books to buy. The evidence appears to be that buying books through school is an activity which remains significant only to the end of the lower secondary stage, at which point young readers begin to make independent choices beyond the school environment.

Although a large proportion of young readers indicate that they buy books in bookshops the picture revealed in the interviews is less clear and in some cases contradicts the survey evidence. Many children stated they did not buy books because of the cost:

> No, you won't find me in a bookshop. They're too expensive...the library I think is much better. (*13-year-old girl*)

Others feel that it is only worth owning books that you might want to re-read:

> Once I've read a book, unless it's a really good one I don't usually read it again so I don't buy many books...but I buy diary books. (*12-year-old girl*)

Keen readers are increasingly independently-minded and are not happy about being given books as gifts:

> I'd much rather have the money for books to choose myself instead of having them given to me. (*12-year-old girl*)

Family influence is clearly a strong factor here. Paradoxically the most independent readers appear to come from homes where families intervene the most in reading habits. Patterns of buying emerge, with several young readers talking about buying books at specific times, notably holidays. At times this extends to what amounts to compulsory book buying:

> Instead of giving me money to buy a book they'll take me into a bookshop and say, right, choose a book and then they'll buy it. And then if we're going away and there won't be anything to do in the evening or something, we'll go out and buy a book each or something like that. (*15-year-old boy*)

The evidence of the discussions shows that most of the respondents are referring to chain bookshops when they talk about their book buying. None of them refers specifically to independent bookshops and some mention the fact that they have no bookshop locally. This may be because the image of the small individually run bookshop does not appeal to older children. One owner of a small independent bookshop said that she had tried without success to entice teenage readers into her shop. A scheme to paint the 'For Older Readers' section in dark colours and with murky lighting, with music to match, as opposed to the pastels of the nursery shelves, seemed to present a possible conflict, so her dilemma remains unresolved. In this specialist children's bookshop the majority of purchasers are parents buying for their children and hardly any older readers come alone to choose.

The only shop mentioned by name is W. H. Smith, by a girl who pragmatically uses it for research purposes (presumably before heading for the library):

> I go round Smith's quite a lot, because I'm always looking for new books, especially now the summer's coming up because I always seem to read more in the holidays...I don't really buy, I just look out for the new books.... (*15-year-old girl*)

Booksellers are working hard to attract more children into the stores. Chains such as W. H. Smith, Dillons and Waterstones have put considerable thought into developing this area, although it is clear that sales to children are as much about marketing as about promoting children's literature. The job descriptions of 'marketing and communications manager for children's interests' and 'promotions manager for children's products' show that the growth area extends beyond books. Dillons have recently extended their children's departments, making them more 'interactive' with the addition of video screens, bean bags and bright lights. All of this is clearly intended to appeal to younger children and their parents. The success of the strategy is clear with rapidly increasing sales. However, in the week before Christmas 1995 the top three selling books in W. H. Smith were *The Goosebumps Book* with free torch, by R. L. Stine, already popular from the *Point Horror* series, the *Funfax Binder* which is a personal organiser for children with puzzles and quizzes and the Disney publication, *The Pocohontas Read Along*. None of these would be described as examples of 'quality' literature. In itself that may not be a problem. It is often said that the aim of early reading should be to get children interested in books and then they will gradually acquire the taste for more demanding or 'worthy' texts. As yet this tendency is not reflected in many children's departments. For the buyer who gravitates away from the attractions of the shelves filled with bright picture books and readers for younger children, the contrast with the section for older readers tends to be dispiriting. Very often it will consist of a small space dominated by *Sweet Valley High,* by *Point Horror, Point Crime* and *Point Romance* and by many volumes of *Babysitter Club.*

Overall, then, although the expressed enthusiasm of the young readers in the survey for buying their own books is to be welcomed, a closer look at the evidence suggests that the picture is not so straightforward. Children and young people clearly enjoy buying and collecting books but not all have the same opportunities to do so and it would be dangerous to assume that increased book sales reflect greater awareness of a range of books and writers; indeed the reverse may be true.

FINDING OUT ABOUT BOOKS

The *Salon du Livre de Jeunesse* held in Montreux, Paris, is an annual event. In 1994 it attracted 140,000 visitors to an exhibition of children's books at which every French publisher who produces books for children is represented, together with authors, illustrators, journalists and TV and radio reporters. The *Salon* is not a trade fair. It is attended by the public in large numbers, including 28,000 teachers and librarians and 32,000 children. These are impressive statistics and are not matched by any event in Britain. It suggests that publishing for children has a different status in other European countries than is the case here. In the UK, writing for children is possibly seen as being a less than serious exercise. For evidence one might cite the experience of Jill Paton Walsh. Acclaimed as a writer for children, and recipient of many prestigious awards including the Whitbread Prize, the literary establishment greeted her adult novel *Knowledge of Angels* with great scepticism and she was compelled to publish it herself before seeing it on the Booker shortlist. Consequently it is not always easy, particularly for non-specialists, to develop a knowledge of children's books.

Reviews of children's books in the broadsheet press tend to be minimal or segregated in occasional special sections, aimed at parents rather than a general readership. The regular updates on children's literature and particularly fiction to be found in journals such as *Books for Keeps, Children's Literature in Education* or *Bookbird,* or the reading lists produced by the Book Trust tend to reach a specialist audience of those professionally involved with children's reading. There is of course material which reaches a more general audience: *Treasure Islands,* the BBC Radio 4 programme introduced by Michael Rosen, achieved the status of being given a Christmas Special on the theme of food in literature for children. Publicity attached to prizes such as the Whitbread or the Smarties Awards reaches adults in the general press (albeit often packaged in controversial rather than celebratory ways). Children may become aware of the award-winning books through the medium of television programmes such as *Blue Peter* or a smaller audience admittedly through radio adaptations. Teen magazines carry reviews of books that may appeal to their readers and for the younger age group a massive amount of publicity is generated by film and TV tie-ins through every possible medium including toys, food items, birthday cards, sweets and stickers. For some they may eventually lead to an encounter with a book. It is worth remembering, however, that in spite of this apparent wealth of choice that the wail still sometimes goes up, 'But I can't find anything to read...' and that it is not safe to assume that all children have equal access to the books they need.

RECOMMENDATIONS

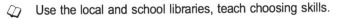 Use the local and school libraries, teach choosing skills.

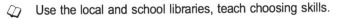 Don't be complacent about library provision, campaign against cuts.

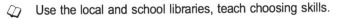 Display books attractively.

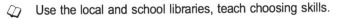 Be aware of which young readers have limited access to books at home.

 Keep up to date on publishing initiatives and use the wide range of resources available to maintain your knowledge of children's literature.

7

Covers and Packaging

Well, I'd look at the front cover. I'd just see which bit stands out and then I'd read the blurb on the back. (*12 year old on being asked how they pick a new author*)

It is widely accepted that the cover of any book is a significant selling point. The cover is an intricate piece of advertising and for many novels it is the first thing to attract the reader's eye. From looking at the front cover, the reader will often turn to the back and read the blurb. The blurb may provide a synopsis of the story and/or different reviews. In design terms the important aspects of the cover are the style, the layout and the typography. All of these features reflect the period in which the cover was designed; the story, however, will stay the same as when it was written. Covers change to keep up-to-date with fashion and thus to attract the reader. 'Compared with the book, the jacket is short lived, it must arouse interest, inform and induce to buy.' (Weidemann 1969) Covers change according to time and culture; as the book is reprinted, so the cover will change. If the book is published by another publisher, the cover will change; if a film is made of the book the new cover would represent this and so on. All publishers realise how important the cover is for marketing purposes and a great deal of thought and energy is put into the design as a result.

Unlike mature readers, young fluent readers do not know the full range of authors available to them. Authors such as Roald Dahl and Dick King-Smith are well known, but there are many more to choose from. Adults and friends often give guidance on what to read, but it seems that when children are making an independent choice they often rely on the front cover to guide them. The following statistics from the survey reflect how influential the cover is in relation to book choice. Of the Key Stage 2 children interviewed, the following stated that they sometimes, often or very often choose a book because they 'like the look of the cover':

Influence of cover on book choice (%)	
Year 3 (8 year olds) 83.1 Year 4 (9 year olds) 75.6	Year 5 (10 year olds) 81.5 Year 6 (11 year olds) 81.1

These amazing statistics show how influential the visual representation of a story is on whether a child will choose a book or not. One 11-year-old girl quite clearly outlines how she chooses a book from the local library: 'I just go through which ones have got a good cover.'

However, even though the front cover is important to primary age children, some readers did realise the need not to depend on it entirely in making their choice:

Girl 1 – I don't think you should depend on front covers, because if you just see a front cover that you like, you buy it and it might not be interesting.
Girl 2 – Yes. If I like the front cover....
Teacher – So what do you look at?
Girl 1 – I look at, like, you know how there's a book and there's a book...and it doesn't say on the front page, but inside it will say what the book's all about, and I read that.
Boy – Yes. If I think the front cover's good then I look at the back. (*11 year olds*)

The 'blurb' or the information about the book on the back or inside the front cover becomes progressively more important as children become older. By the age of eleven over 75% of all children interviewed in the survey said that they chose books because the blurb made the story sound interesting, as this discussion between a group of 11 year olds illustrates:

Girl – I like any book that I find interesting. I just look at the...you know where it says...tells you about a bit on the front page.
Boy 1 – The blurb.
Boy 2 – I always read the back of the...
Girl – ...Yes, the back of the page. And if I find it interesting I just get it really.
Boy 1 – Sometimes I read the back of the blurb, and if I don't like it, then I just put it back. When I come to the library, I read the back of the blurb and if I don't like it I put it back, and then when I find a good one I just take it.

Just what is it that makes a book cover appealing for older primary age children? Nearly 79% said that they chose a book sometimes, often or very often because they liked the pictures on the cover. However, not surprisingly, the older the child the more importance was placed on up-to-date or modern covers; of the 8-year-old children surveyed 59.1% said they sometimes, often or very often chose a book because the cover looked up-to-date, compared with 72.7% 11-year-old children. As children near their teens, so fashion, clothes, music and graphics, become more important and will undoubtedly influence them. Such symbols are important to life and identity, and as a child is nearing adulthood so the search for identity will become stronger. Thus a child nearing their teens, or a teenager, will look for something in a cover that reflects themselves. Nearly 82% of all secondary age pupils surveyed felt that they read a particular book because it looked up-to-date or modern. This, then, strongly reflects the need to stay abreast of modern design trends in the field of children's, and juvenile, book publishing.

However, it has been argued that the covers of juvenile fiction do not keep abreast of their counterparts on CDs and record sleeves. Joanna Carey of *The Guardian* (1994) says:

> Why are so many books for older children obliged to wear dreary jackets? You'd never guess the diversity of fiction they conceal. In the record industry courting the same group of kids, there is no shortage of adventurous, innovative artwork and typography, as there is in graphic art in TV, video and advertising.

As the pupils enter secondary school, book covers are still seen to be an important factor in the readers personal book choice and 85.5% of 14 year olds surveyed said they sometimes, often or very often choose a book because of the cover. However by the age of 16 the percentage had dropped to 77% of pupils. Other factors had begun to play a part in their choice. As children mature in age and reading ability they also begin to realise that the front cover does not represent the whole story; that it is only one person's interpretation of the story in visual form. Choosing by the cover does not suddenly disappear, but what occurs is the ability to articulate the process of choice, as stated by another 12-year-old girl:

> If it looks like a boring book at the front, I won't read it, even if it might be a quite good book inside the cover of the book.

This near-teenager is beginning to realise that the cover is not the complete story, but understanding of the process is not strong enough to deter her from being influenced. Thus if a book has an unattractive, boring or old-fashioned cover she will not read it. This may relate to peer group pressure, what might her peers think if she is seen to be reading a boring looking book! While this 12-year-old reader is making book choices through covers other 12-year-olds seem to have moved on and perhaps use the cover illustrations to helps them get into a story and fill in the gaps in the narrative:

> ...the expressions on the people's faces in the drawings are nice...
> because it helps you understand more of the story.

From the stage of purely looking at the images on the front, and using these in their reading of the story, other 12-year-old pupils seemed to move onto making a decision by looking at the front and then the back cover:

> Well, most of the books I read are, sort of, teenager's. Most of the girls...and when you look at them they've got the sort of things which make you want to read them. And you know, when you read the blurb you think well, obviously somebody's put some work into this. They really want you to read this. And I think I read them because I find them interesting and I can relate to what goes on in them. You know, you could picture it.

The strength of the appeal of an interesting cover for a particular audience is very strong. The 12-year-old girl is being attracted by images and writing aimed at her, her age, gender and interests. The marketing department have achieved their aim, matching a particular book to its reader. The design of a book cover can have a strong appeal for the reader and can virtually demand that it is picked up and looked at, as described by this 13-year-old boy:

> One day I was just looking around a bookshop, I was looking around for any old book and this cover just picked me up straight away. I just went straight to it. I read the back of it and it was just the book for me!

This teenage reader identified very strongly with the ideology illustrated on the cover of the book. Whatever attracted him to the book he felt it was part of his persona, 'it was just the book for me!'. It would be interesting to discuss in depth why he felt the cover, blurb and story were so particular to him. Although, in the field of publishing, we have moved away from identifying explicitly whether a book is for girls or boys – the image, colours, title on the cover, all tell the reader who exactly it is aimed at. As pupils become older so some of them become more particular about the gender representations on the cover, and their choice is strongly influenced by this. But as this 13-year-old boy found out a cover does not always represent the story truthfully:

> The cover on that [*Red Sky in the Morning*] wasn't interesting. It was, kind of, more for girls than for boys. But you had to read it to know that it wasn't... it gave the wrong impression.

However, as the following 13-year-old boy points out, interest, for some readers, can override gender specifications. Paul has an interest in dogs and reads books with dogs in the story, *Puppies in the Pantry*:

> *Teacher* –   That one has got two dogs on the front of it and that has brought you into it but it has also got a girl on the front of it. Did that in any way put you off wanting to read it because you are a boy?
> *Paul* –   No.

As the pupils interviewed became older, reading of the blurb played an important part in the book choice. However, in the survey it was found that the blurb was more important for girls rather than boys. Eighty-four and a half per cent of the secondary age girls surveyed said the blurb sometimes, often or very often influenced them in their choice of reading matter, in comparison with 68.9% of boys.

> But other times I like the look of a book and read the back and if it's quite interesting then I'll read it. (*13-year-old girl*)

Children are also influenced by the covers of books in a series. This is because they know what to look for, as usually the covers are in the same format. A series such as *Point Horror*, published by Scholastic, attracts the young reader because it is brash and bright. This is reflected partly by the following discussion between a 13-year-old boy and girl:

> *Boy* –   I like them [*Point Horrors*] because they're all about teenagers and stuff. The best one I've read is *Funhouse*; it was scary basically all the way through.
> *Girl* –   The cover's as good as well.

It is not just the cover that is important for the teenage reader but what the book looks like overall – whether it is new or old, hardback or paperback. The latter is an issue in public libraries at the present time, in relation to cost and also in rating attractiveness to the reader. The following illustrates how this 13-year-old boy feels about hardbacks:

> Well, I look at the back to see what they've written...maybe it's a hardback...it's an old, probably boring book.

As the pupils became older it did seem that they were able to overcome an initial dislike of a cover and by reading the blurb, inside page or the first page they realised that the book was better than the front cover suggested:

> A book I really enjoyed was *Ginger's First Kiss*. From the cover I thought 'Oh it looks boring' and then I had a look at the first page...so I started reading, and I still thought it was a bit boring, but as I got into it it got more interesting. (*16-year-old girl*)

Thus the older the reader the more they were able to move away from the surface advertising of the cover and use other devices for making book choice, as these GCSE students explain:

> *Girl 1* – If I'm at the library I can read the summary of the story in the front of the book or the back of the book.
> *Teacher* – How do you choose your books?
> *Girl 2* – Usually by what it says on the back of the book and the front, or by recommendation from friends.
> *Teacher* – How important is the jacket to your choice of books?
> *Girl 2* – Not really important because it doesn't really express what's actually in the book. Well, sometimes it doesn't and you can't really tell what's in the book or anything. And if it's a different colour scheme, really bright you know, and you don't go for that kind of thing...you just really go for the words.
> *Girl 1* – I tend to look at the book's cover before I read it, which isn't very good, but I've always done it, even though the amount of times I've been told not to. If a book has no cover on it, it's just plain red or something, I wouldn't look at it. I mean I'd see it, but I wouldn't attempt to look at it. However if a book has a bright jolly...title, I go for the title as well.

Identified here is another important factor for book choice, the title. Thus for some readers, whether they are 9 or 16 years old, the title may also be the initial attraction:

> Well, if I choose it because it's interesting, or the title might sound a bit interesting, like *Street Kids* or *The Angel of . . . [Nitshill Road]* (*9-year-old girl*)

All readers, to a certain extent, are attracted in the same way. The process of choosing books seems to imply a series of steps which allow the story to come through for the reader. Walking into a bookshop, looking for a holiday read, one's eyes rest on the table of bestsellers by the door. At a glance the design, colour and titles fill the vision and then we, the reader, home in on one, pick it up, turn it over in our hands, read the blurb, look for any signs of awards, look inside the cover and so on. The first book picked up may not be the right one and so we put it down and pick up another. There is nothing wrong with this type of book choice, if this is only part of our choosing process. Readers need to use a variety of strategies to identify their reading matter, through recommendation, reading reviews and links to film or television versions. But when the reader is choosing a book in the library or the bookshop an important point to remember is not to be put off by the age of the book, the design on the cover, or the title, but to read all the features to get the real flavour of the story and to see if it really will be a good read for the individual. Perhaps, as adults, we need to teach children to do this from an early age!

RECOMMENDATIONS

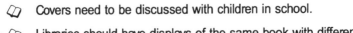

- Covers need to represent the story truly.
- Covers need to be discussed with children in school.
- Libraries should have displays of the same book with different covers.
- Children need to be encouraged to look at the blurb and the beginning of books.

8

Serial Reading

Ask many adults still hooked on books about their childhood reading and memories of Blyton's *Famous Five* or the *Biggles* books will often be recalled. No matter how much the older generation try to persuade children to abandon such books for ones of higher literary merit, the popularity of series books continues. Appleyard (1990, page 85) analyses their appeal:

> Conventional values, type characters, simple plots and one-sided ideals are exactly what 10 or 11 year olds expect to find in stories. Indeed they are what they need to find in them if the stories are to be at all satisfying or meaningful to them, because this is the way the world looks as far as they have succeeded in putting it together for themselves.

Many of the youngest children interviewed testify to this. One 9-year-old boy says that he usually goes for series books because he knows that there's always another to read. He likes the Hardy books because there are 'ninety odd' of them. He rejects other books because he is worried that if he likes it too much, there won't be another to continue the pleasure. This sentiment is echoed by a girl of the same age:

> Yes. There's something about some books, you know, you don't particularly want them to be, like, continued in a separate book, but you wish they were like in a series.

However another girl of 9 feels differently:

> But the ones in the series, don't seem to be ... they don't always seem to be as good as the actual singular books.

Perhaps one of the most valuable aspects of series books for this age is that they can be the start of a child's breakthrough into reading independently. A case study of an 8 year old illustrates the phenomena. Up until his eighth birthday, this child had been an avid *Beano* reader and liked non-fiction texts but he had shown no real interest in reading story books on his own. Then one of his friends gave him a *Goosebumps* book for his birthday.

Perhaps because it was a present from a friend, he read it and loved it. Not only was he pleased that he could now join the group of *Goosebump* fans but he began to feel that he had something to collect, in the way that he had previously collected football stickers and 'pogs'. He wanted to know how many there were in the full set and what order they came in. His mother had to make a list and he started to count them off as they read them. He bought some and he borrowed others from his friends. Buying them was easy because he knew where to find them even in large bookshops. As he says:

> They are easy to find because they say *Goosebumps* out loud. When I see other sets of books like the *Babysitters Club* then I know they are going to be there.

He became part of a club – 'all my friends read them' – and the security of knowing what he is getting every time he picks up a new title has helped to make him a reader.

The popularity of series books certainly continues into the lower end of the secondary school as this exchange shows:

> *Girl –* I like the *Babysitter* books and *Sweet Valley High* books. I enjoy series of books.
> *Teacher –* Why do you like series books?
> *Girl –* Because you can, once you've finished a book and you've found it really good, you can always go back and get another and another and it will be really good as well.

Another 11-year-old girl describes why she reads so many series books:

> I like Enid Blyton's series of *Malory Towers* and the *Sweet Valley High* ones and the *Babysitter* ones because with Enid Blyton's school books they end with 'we'll see about it next term' and then you're thinking, I've got to read about next term because they've played all these tricks and I've got to read about that and with the *Babysitter* ones the phone is about to ring and that and then you close the book and you're thinking, who's picked up the phone. With the *Sweet Valley High*, it's really good because it says things like next week find out about it in book no. 23, find out Amy's true love, to see what's happened. They leave it at the dead end and then you just have to read on.

Other interviews show how girls feel that these books prepare them for approaching situations:

> *Teacher –* Why do you think these books are so popular? Why do you

think people like *Sweet Valley High* and *Babysitters Club*?
Girl 1 – Because it's about school life and real things happening.
Teacher – What sort of things?
Girl 1 – Well in the *Sweet Valley High*, they have the Unicorn clubs
and school work and it's about school newspapers and what everyone
would do at school. It's like real life drama. Whereas in some story
books, ordinary story books like *Thomas the Tank Engine* you don't see
that happening.
Girl 2 – The new book I've bought, from [*The Boyfriend Club* series],
it's got Ginger's first kiss, like it would have happened, like our age – it's
going to happen sometime – it's going to tell us what's going to happen
(*collapses in giggles*).

The enthusiasm for what is easily recognisable as a series book appears to
diminish as pupils progress through the secondary school. One 14-year-old
girl reader values variety at this stage:

When I was younger my favourite was Roald Dahl. But now I sort of
like to hop around. Because basically if one author has a really good
book, and then you read another one...in a series, and it's not very
good at all, so you can go off them. So I can hop around basically to
different authors.

A 13-year-old girl is more blunt:

I don't really like horror any more. I've gone off...I don't like *Point
Horror*. They've all got the same storyline.

Other commentators who assess teenager reading, support the notion that
the appeal of series books wears off at this stage. David Bennett, in a *Books
for Keeps* article, observes:

Where teenagers are concerned, you definitely can't always rely on serial
reading to keep the pages turning. After the first flush of enthusiasm and
roughly three or four titles, the novelty wears off in favour of
alternatives. (*Issue 90, January 1995*)

Appleyard believes that as readers grow older, they become more interested
in character:

So they look for stories about people who are not simply good or bad,
stories about intentions and motives and points of view and how they

might conflict even in well-meaning people. In short, their own role as readers changes and the attitudes toward stories that satisfied them as juveniles no longer work for them as adolescents.

This is really where there is a challenge for adults who want to keep teenagers reading. If series books can help emerging readers get going, guidance and support is needed when series books lose their grip. Parents worry unnecessarily if their 11 year olds are devouring all the *Point Horrors* available. What's much worse is when they lose interest in this diet and are unable to find books to fill the gap. Teenagers are not well served when it comes to reading. Their magazines do not promote books, there is nothing informative on television and very few adult publications give any guidance.

All age groups agree about why they think they like series books. When given six possible reasons for choosing to read books in a series, the most popular choice for all ages of girls and boys was that they liked reading about the same characters. For example, over 72% of girls felt this was the reason that they often or very often read books in a series and the percentage for boys is almost as high. Perhaps even more interesting than this is the *least* popular reason for reading series books. Again, nearly all the respondents across the age range and gender distribution gave a similar rating to the possibility that they read these books because they knew what to expect in the story. Girls, in particular, seem willing to reject this reason with no more than 39% of girls at any age choosing this option. This finding does not sit very easily with the commonly-held view that it is the familiarity of what to expect which is so appealing about series books. Perhaps it is unfair to expect all children to recognise this appeal while still caught up in it. It could be that it is mainly as adults reflecting on their reading that they can recognise what the appeal was. Inglis (1981) talks about his own childhood reading of Enid Blyton's series books:

> Partly I read them for utter unreality. The adventures were such as to hurt no one, and I wanted to be sure of painlessness. Partly I read them for the untaxing safety of their stereotypes...Indeed I was hardly troubled by the notion of 'character' at all. I wanted the placid, predictable turn and return of events...

One type of series reading, of which the *Goosebumps* and *Point Horror* titles already mentioned are prime examples, has been getting a vast amount of publicity recently. It seems that not a week goes by without some newspaper article appearing which tries to analyse the hold of horror stories on the youth of today. This is not new. They have been causing comment among the adult population for many years. As long ago as the 1950s, P. M. Pickard's (1961) research into horror, violence and sensationalism in stories for children looked at both the appeal and the disquiet produced by this kind of fiction. Pickard concluded that left to their own devices, young people tended to enjoy the excitement of frightening fiction (and girls in particular enjoyed the active life it pictured), but disliked the consequences of reading too much or too graphic material of this sort. Certainly, the survey supports the widely-held view that horror is the most popular genre in secondary schools. Nearly 65% of girls and 52.9% of boys across this age range responded that they read a substantial amount of horror stories. The peak of its popularity is when pupils are 12 and 13 years old. Seventy-one per cent of 13-year-old girls said that they often or very often read horror stories. The picture in primary schools is different. For girls, adventure (57.7%), funny (65.3%) and animal (56.1%) stories are all more popular than horror (49.8%), while for the boys horror (59.3%) comes third behind adventure (67.3%) and funny (61.8%) stories. The appeal of horror for girls only starts as they reach the end of the primary school. Indeed, 61.3% of 7-year-old girls responded negatively to reading horror books while 60.2% of 11 year olds replied positively. However, there is little difference in the response of boys from 7 to 11 years old.

One 10-year-old girl who was interviewed for the survey tries to explain her enjoyment of horror stories. She likes them because 'they go slowly and so she doesn't know what is going to happen'. She mainly reads *Point Horrors* and is able to compare writers. She, like many others, thinks R. L. Stine is one of the best *Point Horror* writers so she has not only a series to follow but also a writer. She recognises that it is because they are fiction that she can enjoy them safely:

> I prefer fiction books. Because some of the *Point Horrors*, they can get scary, and if they're fiction . . . because if it was non-fiction people would be getting freaked out all the time.

There is some evidence from the interviews that the adults asking the questions are surprised by some of the answers they get. This interview with a 10-year-old boy is interesting.

Teacher – Horror books? So what makes a good horror book?
Boy – Well you've got the hero in the bathroom having a shower, and someone comes up with a knife to stab you.
Teacher – Oh. Are they children's horror books?
Boy – Yes.

Teacher – So what kind of horror books are they, then?

Boy – My sister buys them and I borrow them from her.

Teacher – So are they grown-up or just books meant for older children?

Boy – Books meant for older children.

Teacher – Right. So, what's good about them then? That's it... you said about being in the shower and someone coming behind you. I presume that means in the story? So what... does that make you feel when you read that?

Boy – Scared!

The series horror books, of which Scholastic's *Point Horrors* are the most popular, are certainly marketed for their scare appeal. Covers which scream at you, 'You have been warned' and 'A one way ticket... to terror' are not promising cosy stories. Even the *Goosebumps* for the younger readers are playing on the idea of fear. The 9 year old described earlier in this chapter was well aware of the importance of this aspect of the books:

The titles are good – they sound good and on the cover it has an important message: 'Reader beware, you're in for a scare'. They really are, you know. They scare you out of your pants.

Older children also comment on the 'scare' quality of *Point Horror* titles but one girl's comments are interesting. First of all she describes how scared she was when her mother read *Little Red Riding Hood* to her as a small child. She was so scared that her mother had to stop reading it to her and when it was read at her nursery school, she had to be taken home. Yet, immediately after describing these remembered feelings, she announces that she is a *Point Horror* addict. When asked to explain why these books do not scare her in the same way, she just says they are different. Perhaps Charles Sarland's conclusions (1994) about the appeal of this series for 12 year olds helps here. He believes that it is the 'representation of the dramas and tribulations of teenage life that speaks with particular effectiveness.' He also concludes that these young readers are asking questions about what it is to be a teenager and what it means to transgress. Certainly another 12 year old's comment that 'They aren't really scary, but it's nice to think they are,' suggests that the main appeal of *Point Horrors* is ultimately *not* to be 'scared out of your pants'. Perhaps some of the older readers who really want to be scared have to turn to stronger stuff. This 12-year-old girl clearly shocks her interviewer with her choice of book:

Teacher –   Have you managed to find anything recently to make you inspired?

Girl –   I quite liked *The Silence of the Lambs*.

Teacher –   Gosh, that's a book that you wouldn't normally expect somebody of your age to be reading. Do your Mum and Dad know you've been reading that? I bet that's one you read under the bedcovers (*laughs*). Right. Does your Mum know you're reading it? It's alright, I'm not going to rush off and telephone her (*laughs*).

Girl –   Yes, she does.

Teacher –   Right. It's very difficult book to read. Do you understand it?

Girl –   Yes.

There is little adults can do if they are disturbed by the idea of a 12 year old enjoying a book about a man who relishes eating human flesh with a drop of Chianti. An imaginative response to a child who does favour the horrible is to widen their knowledge of this type of text. Of course, Shakespeare has some gruesome scenes but he is not the answer for private reading. *Frankenstein* perhaps in the latest adaptation by Robin Waterfield (1994), is an idea as are the short stories of Edgar Allen Poe and Guy de Maupassant. Several of Robert Westall's stories for older readers include horror. But if Stephen King is the author who keeps them turning the pages, then it seems counterproductive to be shocked. Series books clearly encourage reading. This has always been the case and the survey and interviews shed some light on the attraction of a book that belongs to a set. It is how to encourage reading once the appeal begins to fade that should be the prime concern of anyone involved with reading.

RECOMMENDATIONS

- Allow young children, particularly boys, to discuss and share their *Goosebump* titles.

- Don't rubbish their choices – get them to talk about their appeal.

- Help children to consider alternatives if they are reading a very limited range of books.

- Find out about suitable books for teenagers who no longer want to read serial books.

9

Feelings about Reading

That's the best thing you can ever do is read.

READING IN THE JUNIOR SCHOOL (KEY STAGE 2)

Unselfconscious enthusiasm for reading, such as that expressed by this young reader quoted above is guaranteed to delight the teacher and is happily frequently apparent among the responses from the children surveyed in Key Stage 2. Among the keen readers in the survey of this age group there is a strong sense of the pleasure to be had in reading. This enjoyment is directed equally at fiction and non-fiction material and across a range of contexts for reading both at home and in school. Boys and girls expressed themselves equally keen on reading as an activity.

Some of the Key Stage 2 readers appear to be developing a strong sense of themselves as readers. One girl says 'I'm kind of getting addicted to books'. Another girl refers to reading as 'one my best hobbies'. It may not be reading too much into these and similar statements to suggest that for these young readers (both 9 years old) there is a powerful sense of pride and achievement in acquiring reading skills that may match other milestones, such as learning to ride a bicycle or to swim. Autonomy in reading is felt to be a marker of increasing independence and maturity as they move from the infant to junior phase. Some, at least, are achieving a fluency in reading which permits them the experience of 'getting lost' in the book. Where there is access to a range of books, enthusiasm and motivation are high:

Well like I said, *Jasper*, that's a really exciting book to read. You just want to turn the page. You can't stop reading. You want to see what happens.

Reading is seen as an exciting option: 'If you get bored... if you're really into a book you just want to finish it up.'

Some young readers are becoming analytical about the experience of reading. For example, two children considered the differences between reading and the attractions of the computer. On balance, reading was preferable, they suggested, on account of the portability of a book: 'You can't take a computer around with you...you can settle down anywhere with a book and start reading' (*11-year-old boy*).

There are other instances of pragmatic approaches to reading skills. Children in the junior phase are aware that reading experience is necessary in order to further their own developing language skills. Some refer explicitly to the idea that reading will increase their vocabulary or understanding of topics. Reading is seen, therefore, as being not only an enjoyable leisure activity but as one which is likely to contribute to knowledge and understanding, at a time in their lives when young readers are highly receptive to new information. At the same time they appear to have an explicit understanding that reading is likely to contribute to academic success, that reading is important 'when you're doing exams and stuff' as one child put it.

While there are many responses which indicate positive attitudes to reading there are already signs that for some children reading is problematic. The pleasure in story persists from younger days, with such comments as: 'I like listening to stories but not reading them' (*9-year-old girl*) being a typical response. A significant number of the children said that they read less as they got older. There are a whole range of reasons for this: access to books, different emphasis in the curriculum, pressure from other activities. One possibly significant reason offered from a 10 year old was that 'When I was younger the books were easier.'

For some readers it is apparent that the gap between their maturity and understanding and their reading skills begins to open at a relatively early age. The same boy suggested that there were fewer books to choose from now. Objectively this was a false perception on his part, but he was expressing his sense that there were fewer books available at his level of understanding, when he went on to say that to him 'All the books look the same...you don't get lots of pictures for my age reading group.'

He becomes bewildered by the choices open to him once the support of illustrations is no longer there. Paradoxically it seems that while some young readers are excited by the possibilities of the range of material they see opening up before them, there are others who cannot make sense of the choices available and so they fail to establish an identity as an independent reader.

In an interesting exchange with his teacher this boy is pressed to say why he does not read a great deal:

Teacher – Be honest, I'm not going to tell you off.
Boy – (*Hesitates*) Well, I'm not very good at reading.

While being specific to a particular relationship between teacher and pupil, this certainly has wider significance. It locates reading firmly as an activity which is potentially problematic, even associated explicitly by the teacher with the possibility of punishment for failure to progress. This, alongside the other comments related to reading for projects and topic work, suggests that many children at this stage are beginning to see reading as a pastime that is sanctioned by teachers and associated with success at school rather than being one they would choose for themselves.

KEY STAGE 3

As with the readers in Key Stage 2 the 11 to 14 year olds have a strong sense that reading is a worthwhile activity because it is likely to help them at school. Well over half of the respondents mention that reading would help to extend their vocabulary. Reading is educational, it helps with your spelling, story writing and grammar, it enables you to write in different styles and to succeed in examinations. An 11-year-old girl expresses this notion most strongly when she says firmly, 'If you can't read you can't write and therefore you can't write and therefore you can't do anything really.'

The link between reading and writing which is commonly claimed by these young readers is an interesting one, as lower down the age range the connection between reading and other areas of achievement in school tends to be conveyed in a more general way. It may be safe to conclude it is a view which is suggested by secondary English teachers. It was mildly disappointing to note that only one girl suggested that reading might actually make you a better reader and it is tempting to speculate whether teachers make enough of this link.

A further difference between Key Stage 2 and 3 was that for the older readers the sense of the world of work and the demands of adult life are becoming more apparent. For many of them, the prime purpose of reading is linked to getting a job: pupils of this age are well aware that most jobs require reading skills. They tend, however, to interpret reading skills in limited ways. They talk about having a wide vocabulary or being able to read forms rather than, for instance, conveying any sense that reading for nuance or for bias are important skills. Even more mundanely there is the suggestion that you cannot negotiate the aisles of a supermarket without an ability to read packets and advertisements. Reading is at once an educational activity and one which is worthy in itself because teachers, parents and other figures of authority decree it to be so.

Fortunately there are still a significant proportion who internalise the sense of reading as a pleasurable activity in its own right. From the interviews there is a clear sense that these readers are well aware of a hierarchy: reading books is superior to reading comics, and it is better, as a 13-year-old girl puts it, 'to start appreciating books, instead of sitting in front of the telly all day or reading magazines.'

These readers retain a sense of the entertainment to be gained from books. The word 'fun' is one which they choose frequently to describe their feelings about books. Like the younger readers they have a sense of what is specific to the experience of reading:

> When you're reading you're actually taking it into your head instead of the TV putting it there. (*14-year-old girl*)

Some have a strong sense of particular authors or genres which appeal:

> I thought this is really good; I want to read more by this author, and then you just go on. (*13-year-old girl*)

What is remarkable at this stage is that the divide between readers and non-readers is more pronounced. Whereas in Key Stage 2 there were children who expressed themselves to be uncomfortable about reading, there were responses at Key Stage 3 which were disaffected, with some declaring themselves to 'hate reading'. And those who do not enjoy reading have many other distractions. The transition from primary to secondary phases of education brings with it a range of other opportunities and distractions and frequently a good deal of homework. These activities cut into the time available for reading. Even keen readers report that they do most of their reading at bedtime, while those with negative feelings about books turn to their computers, the television or to activities which take them outside the home.

If there are some who are consciously rejecting reading as a regular habit then others are demonstrating reading patterns and feelings about reading which are the basis of adult reading habits. Where younger children may revel in books for the range of information contained and for portrayals of their own immediate experience and interests, young teenage readers are at a point of transition. Clearly they enjoy books which reflect their own world: *Point Horror* books are cited as being popular because they present teenagers in satisfyingly scary circumstances. Likewise the *Sweet Valley High* series has young people as the protagonists and also link with a fictional world that is familiar from television. Equally at this stage books offer an introduction to the world of adult ideas and experience. A 15-year-old girl puts it like this:

There are ones about older people and you sort of think 'I wonder if that will happen to me?'.

On one level books are useful to support school work or hobbies and other interests. On another level, a sense emerges from the interviews of young people who are beginning to use books to extend their thinking and to give them access to other opinions and points of view. Reading is seen as being an activity which involves and engages rather than being a passive experience. This was expressed interestingly by a 12 year old who suggested that 'when you read something you interpret it in your own way but when someone tells you something it's usually their point of view.'

Another 14-year-old girl who explained that: '...reading helps you if you're around adults, to help speak their sort of language if you want to, because you know more...' is not referring exclusively to features of vocabulary, but is thinking about how books give her an insight into adult ways of seeing the world. For more competent readers, books begin to fulfil an emotional and a psychological need. Another girl talks about how when upset or anxious she turns to books: 'I read, and it calms me down a bit.'

There is a certain coyness, possibly deriving from the interview context, but others are looking to books for information and understanding about areas of their lives that are confusing or embarrassing:

You might not want to ask other people, but you can go off and look for it in a book. (*13-year-old boy*)

KEY STAGE 4

At this stage the distinction between willing and reluctant readers is most pronounced. All of the reasons offered by the 11 to 14 year olds for reading were reinforced by the older age group. With GCSE examinations approaching they are more than ever conscious that it is essential to read in order to ensure success in English and across the range of other subjects being studied. In spite of this general awareness of the significance of reading for their academic success, some of those surveyed stated that they never read at all voluntarily.

Even those who profess themselves keen on reading apparently read relatively little. For example, one 15 year old who talked articulately about books estimated that she had read five books in a term. One practical reason for this is clearly the demands being made upon these young readers by school, wider socialising and other preferred activities such as sport. Reading is a pastime which has to be pursued after many other commitments have been met and this affects the motivation of enthusiastic readers as well as those who rate reading low in their priorities. It is not surprising, perhaps, that there is less evidence from this age group of exploration of the range of writing available to them or of their encountering new authors and genres. Many of those interviewed talked about rereading books they had enjoyed previously, and several refer to reading as being a soothing occupation:

> If I've done a lot of homework and I'm sort of highly strung and stressed out then I read because it relaxes me. (*16-year-old girl*)

Compared with the readers in the Key Stage 3 phase, less antipathy is noted. Whereas some of the younger readers denounced reading, at this stage there is a nostalgic appreciation of texts remembered from early childhood. Adolescent boys reminisced about their encounters with *Postman Pat* and fond memories emerged of Roald Dahl and Enid Blyton.

While some 15 and 16 year olds are happy to define themselves as readers and consciously make time for books in otherwise pressured lives, there are others for whom the experience of enjoying fiction for its own sake is a thing of the past. Memories of bedtime stories, and of the book corner in the primary classroom are relics of childhood and have no place in their adult consciousness. For some young readers there is a continuum of development in reading skills which leaves them not only with the skills they need for adult purposes but also with a habit of reading for pleasure that will continue into adulthood. Many do not, however, for in spite of all of the positive enthusiasm shown by younger readers by the age of 16, as many as 30% of girls and 60% of boys say that they never or hardly ever read fiction for pleasure at all.

Need this concern us? After all, no child is any longer starved of imaginative experience, or of the opportunity to enter a fictional narrative through the medium of film or television. Probably it should. Nicholas Tucker (1981, page 230) puts it like this, first acknowledging the appeal of the visual media, he argues for literature:

> Children today receive from television a greater quantity of ready-made fictional material than at any other time in history. But this outpouring of what is very often stereotyped and repetitive material can eventually start to impose its own restrictions upon the imagination. One strong argument for literature now, therefore, is that it often has the potential to offer a different, far more individual imaginative experience to the child, in which he or she may sometimes discover important personal

meanings unavailable to them elsewhere.

Reading a book is a uniquely 'interactive' experience, be it for information, for relaxation, or for exploring important personal issues. Reading skills remain relevant and significant in terms of personal development in spite of high-tech dissemination of information and rapidly developing visual literacies. The fact that so many of the young readers spoke passionately about their pleasure in books and reading is a cause for pleasure and celebration. The fact that for so many the pleasure in reading is a short-lived phase, is a cause for concern among all of those interested in the young people's reading at the end of the century.

THE SURVEY

Talking about Books

A substantial part of the material gathered to supplement the main survey was in the form of semi-structured interviews carried out by teachers in school. The purpose of the interviews was twofold. They were intended to substantiate the information in the main survey. Secondly and more important, they were intended to allow for more detailed responses than were possible in the questionnaire and to give a more complex insight into the feelings of young readers about books and their reading practices. The interviews were set up by the participating schools following a similar set of broad guidelines.

GUIDELINES FOR THE INTERVIEWS

Schools were asked to choose the participants at random so as to get a range of views. In mixed schools teachers were asked to attempt to get a balance of boys and girls. The interviews took place a day or two after the questionnaires were completed, so that those ideas were still fresh in the minds of the interviewees. As for the time allotted, the interviews were quite brief: the suggestion was 10–20 minutes. It was suggested that teachers might prefer to carry out the interviews, as this is an excellent way of finding out more about pupil's reading. If this was not possible it was suggested that a librarian, a support teacher or even a parent would be an appropriate person. It was recommended that a quiet corner in the library or an office would be the best place to carry out the interviews as the classroom would offer too many distractions. The schedule of questions was provided, but teachers were free to raise the topics in any order, and to word them as they saw fit. All of the interviews were tape recorded and subsequently transcribed for the NCRCL. The full interview schedule for Key Stage 2 (8–11 year olds) is included here in full. The schedule for the older pupils was substantially the same although they were also asked for their opinions of the questionnaire.

Questionnaire

1. Do you like reading? How much time do you spend reading? Is it important to you and if so can you say why? Do you read more or less than you used to?

2. Did you have a bedtime story when you were younger? Can you remember any stories that were read to you? Do you ever read to someone younger than yourself?

3. When do you read? Is there a time in school for quiet reading? Do you like reading your own books in school? Is it easy to find somewhere to read at home? Where is your best place for reading?

4. Where do you find the books you read? Who helps you choose the books you read? Do your friends help you to choose? Do parents make helpful suggestions? Do you ever read books you have seen on television?

5. How often do you use a library to find books to read? Does the librarian help you to choose your books?

6. Can you tell me about any books you have read recently that you really enjoyed? Are there any authors that you particularly like?

7. Is your reading mostly fiction or non-fiction? If non-fiction, do you read books about other hobbies and interests?

8. Do you use another language? Do you read any books in your own language and if so what kind?

9. How much do you read comics and magazines? Do you enjoy them more than books? Do you have a favourite one?

10. Do you read newspapers? Which newspaper do you like to read? Which sections do you read most?

11. Do you read books or magazines to get information about personal or social issues? Are books or magazines most useful for this kind of information?

AN EVALUATION OF THE INTERVIEWS

The experience gained in carrying out this extensive series of interviews is a potentially useful framework for teachers interested in carrying out similar work with their own classes.

GROUPINGS

A variety of groupings were used by teachers, although most of the interviews took place in groups of three or four. This seemed to work well as pupils reacted to each others' ideas and were willing to talk freely about their experiences. The interviews which involved two pupils were very valuable where they were equally matched in their enthusiasm for books. When one was a keen reader and the other unenthusiastic less useful information was generated. Some teachers opted for one-to-one interviews. On the whole this seemed to be less helpful and tended to generate monosyllabic answers or more predictable replies.

There were interesting observations about the gender mix in groups. Boys in the older age groups noticeably talked more freely in single sex groups than they did when talking with girls. Teachers might bear this in mind when setting up groups to talk about books. Another interesting strategy was to set up peer interviews with pairs of students set to interview each other. The success of this depended on how well they had understood the purpose of the discussion and the questions, but when carried out thoughtfully, these interviews had the potential to elicit as much useful insights into reading as those conducted by teachers.

THE ROLE OF THE INTERVIEWER

All the interviews were carried out by teachers, although not always by the pupil's own regular teacher. Some teachers maintained a neutral stance, no matter how startling the opinions being expressed by the interviewees. On other occasions it was obvious that the teacher found it hard to contain herself, as in this instance when the pupil said that he was forced to read books he did not like:

> I really feel that I've got to put in the opinion of the English teacher here. I mean, I think the reason we do this is that what's supposed to happen is that we open your eyes a little bit...

This seems to be a reasonable intervention. However in some cases teachers seemed to be imposing their views on the interviewees:

> What did you think of the questionnaire? Was it stupid, boring and long winded?

Even less helpful were the interviews, and there were only a few, when the teacher dominated the talk and sometimes even cut off the discussion or stopped a train of thought just at the point when it seemed to be getting interesting. It is important to be aware of the pitfalls of dominating the interview, rather than giving the pupils genuine opportunities to express their ideas.

Using the questions

Some of the teachers worked through the questions in a semi-structured way, apparently checking off the items as they did so. This had the merit of being comprehensive and ensuring that all of the topics were covered. At the other extreme some interviews ranged far from the point. Two pages of transcript gave a fascinating account of the debate between two brothers as to who should clear up after their dog was sick, but it revealed little about their reading attitudes and habits. The most useful strategy for the interviews were those where the teacher allowed the discussion to flow and then intervened occasionally to ask the interviewees to consider a fresh topic or expand on one they had covered previously, according to the prearranged pattern of questions. Above all it is important to focus as much on the answers as the questions. This tension between guiding the interview and at the same time being responsive to the answers can be a difficult one. If possible it can be helpful to enlist the help of others to make notes or to ask the questions. This is not as wildly optimistic as it seems, if parent helpers, student teachers or even sixth formers can be enlisted.

Taping interviews

The survey interviews were taped and then transcribed. This can be a useful technique but is inevitably a hugely time-consuming exercise. The advantage of the technique is that it gives the teacher/researcher the opportunity to reflect on the detail of what has been said, while at the same time avoiding the need to make notes during the interview. However, it is worthwhile taping interviews even if it is not intended to transcribe them in their entirety, although it is always sensible to explain the reasons for doing so to the interviewees. Listening to the tapes after the interviews can often reveal aspects of the discussion which were not immediately apparent. It may then be worthwhile transcribing some parts of the interviews. The interviews can also be incorporated into other classroom activities: interviews such as these would, for instance, provide very useful evidence for National Curriculum assessment or for GCSE literature as well as enhancing the teachers' understanding of the reading development of the members of their classes.

PUPIL PERCEPTIONS

There was a powerful sense that the boys and girls in the interviews enjoyed talking about their reading. In fact they resented being cut short:

Teacher – Thank you for your time, that's about it...
Boy – Hey! that was only five minutes!

Curiously some of them seemed to regard the questionnaire, which was completed anonymously, as being intrusive, while the interviews which were altogether more personal affairs were seen as an enjoyable experience. This is due probably to the fact that the questionnaire asked for details about personal issues at Key Stages 3 and 4, while the interview did not demand responses to every question and the more personal issues were not introduced. What was very clear was that these interviews gave young readers an opportunity to talk about their preferences in a way which was quite unusual in that it moved away from the normal diet of the classroom and picked up on reading habits which sometimes surprised their teachers:

Girl – Oh, and *Vanity Fair*.
Teacher – (*astonished*) You've read *Vanity Fair*? That's amazing because I haven't...

For some of the children who took part, the interviews plainly gave them a chance to reveal to their teacher a range of ideas about books and a sense of themselves as readers which was missing from the normal activities of the classroom.

CONFERENCING AS A STRATEGY FOR READING DEVELOPMENT

It has been a central theme of this study that anyone, be they parent, teacher, librarian, wishing to foster the development of reading as an enriching habit must begin from a sense of the young reader as an *individual*.

All kinds of factors can inhibit that understanding. It was evident from the transcripts of the interviews carried out here that for many of the teachers and pupils taking part this kind of discussion about reading was a novel experience. We hope that one result will be that others will continue these conversations in their own schools, homes and libraries. The interviews which have provided the material for this study were conducted with a particular objective. However, it has long been understood (see the *Primary Language Record* 1990) that what is termed as 'conferencing', that is the practice of sitting down and talking to children about their reading and exploring their ideas about books, can be immensely revealing, not just in increasing the understanding of where the young reader is today but in where she or he might be tomorrow, or in the years to come, given the support and encouragement of an interested adult.

SURVEY RESULTS

Taken from *Young People's Reading at the End of the Century*. Data reproduced by kind permission of the NCRCL, Roehampton Institute London.

Who helps you choose which books to read? Responses to the option: mother

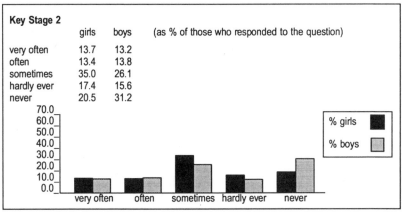

Key Stage 2

	girls	boys	(as % of those who responded to the question)
very often	13.7	13.2	
often	13.4	13.8	
sometimes	35.0	26.1	
hardly ever	17.4	15.6	
never	20.5	31.2	

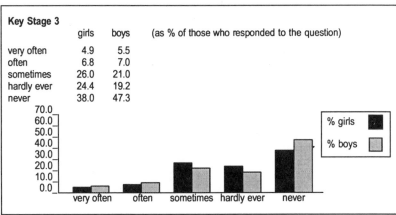

Key Stage 3

	girls	boys	(as % of those who responded to the question)
very often	4.9	5.5	
often	6.8	7.0	
sometimes	26.0	21.0	
hardly ever	24.4	19.2	
never	38.0	47.3	

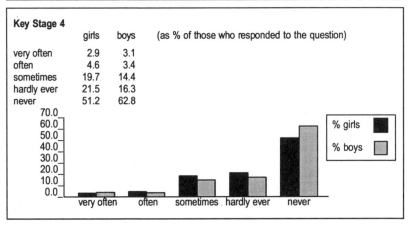

Key Stage 4

	girls	boys	(as % of those who responded to the question)
very often	2.9	3.1	
often	4.6	3.4	
sometimes	19.7	14.4	
hardly ever	21.5	16.3	
never	51.2	62.8	

Who helps you choose which books to read? Responses to the option: father

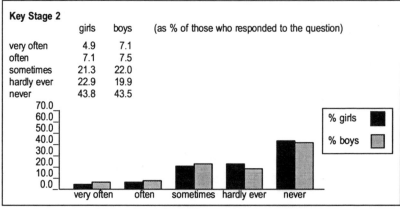

Key Stage 2

	girls	boys	(as % of those who responded to the question)
very often	4.9	7.1	
often	7.1	7.5	
sometimes	21.3	22.0	
hardly ever	22.9	19.9	
never	43.8	43.5	

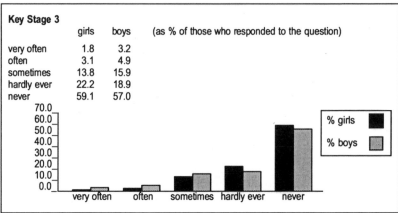

Key Stage 3

	girls	boys	(as % of those who responded to the question)
very often	1.8	3.2	
often	3.1	4.9	
sometimes	13.8	15.9	
hardly ever	22.2	18.9	
never	59.1	57.0	

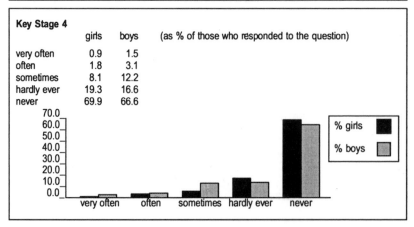

Key Stage 4

	girls	boys	(as % of those who responded to the question)
very often	0.9	1.5	
often	1.8	3.1	
sometimes	8.1	12.2	
hardly ever	19.3	16.6	
never	69.9	66.6	

Who helps you choose which books to read? Responses to the option: friend(s)

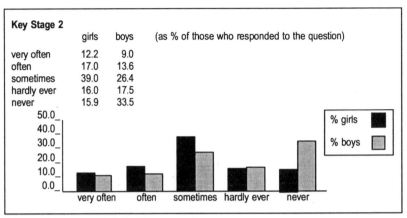

Key Stage 2

	girls	boys	(as % of those who responded to the question)
very often	12.2	9.0	
often	17.0	13.6	
sometimes	39.0	26.4	
hardly ever	16.0	17.5	
never	15.9	33.5	

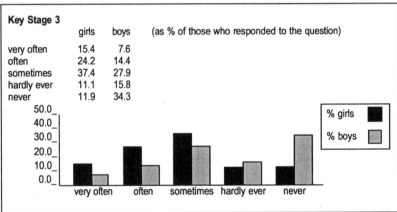

Key Stage 3

	girls	boys	(as % of those who responded to the question)
very often	15.4	7.6	
often	24.2	14.4	
sometimes	37.4	27.9	
hardly ever	11.1	15.8	
never	11.9	34.3	

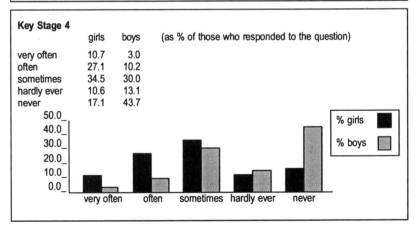

Key Stage 4

	girls	boys	(as % of those who responded to the question)
very often	10.7	3.0	
often	27.1	10.2	
sometimes	34.5	30.0	
hardly ever	10.6	13.1	
never	17.1	43.7	

Who helps you choose which books to read? Responses to the option: teacher(s)

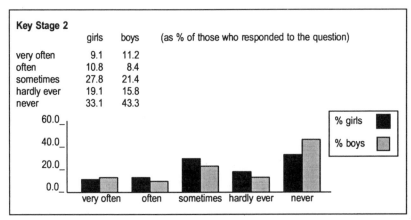

Key Stage 2

	girls	boys	(as % of those who responded to the question)
very often	9.1	11.2	
often	10.8	8.4	
sometimes	27.8	21.4	
hardly ever	19.1	15.8	
never	33.1	43.3	

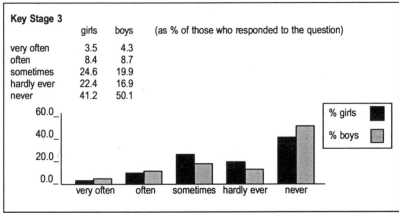

Key Stage 3

	girls	boys	(as % of those who responded to the question)
very often	3.5	4.3	
often	8.4	8.7	
sometimes	24.6	19.9	
hardly ever	22.4	16.9	
never	41.2	50.1	

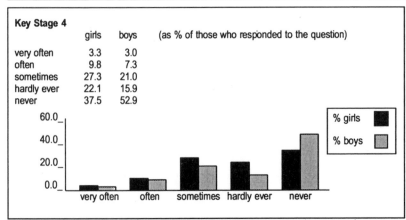

Key Stage 4

	girls	boys	(as % of those who responded to the question)
very often	3.3	3.0	
often	9.8	7.3	
sometimes	27.3	21.0	
hardly ever	22.1	15.9	
never	37.5	52.9	

Who helps you choose which books to read? Responses to the option: local librarian(s)

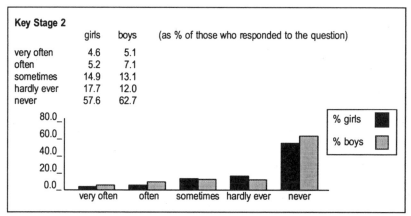

Key Stage 2

	girls	boys	(as % of those who responded to the question)
very often	4.6	5.1	
often	5.2	7.1	
sometimes	14.9	13.1	
hardly ever	17.7	12.0	
never	57.6	62.7	

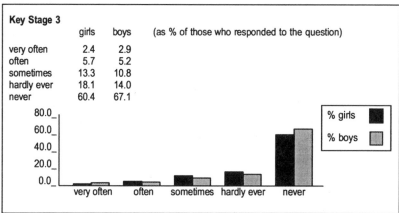

Key Stage 3

	girls	boys	(as % of those who responded to the question)
very often	2.4	2.9	
often	5.7	5.2	
sometimes	13.3	10.8	
hardly ever	18.1	14.0	
never	60.4	67.1	

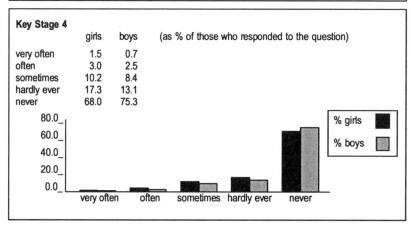

Key Stage 4

	girls	boys	(as % of those who responded to the question)
very often	1.5	0.7	
often	3.0	2.5	
sometimes	10.2	8.4	
hardly ever	17.3	13.1	
never	68.0	75.3	

Who helps you choose which books to read? Responses to the option: school librarian(s)

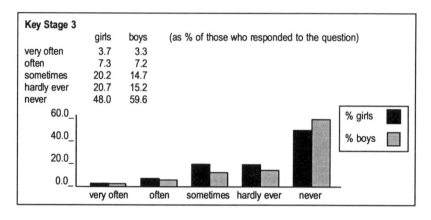

Key Stage 3

	girls	boys	(as % of those who responded to the question)
very often	3.7	3.3	
often	7.3	7.2	
sometimes	20.2	14.7	
hardly ever	20.7	15.2	
never	48.0	59.6	

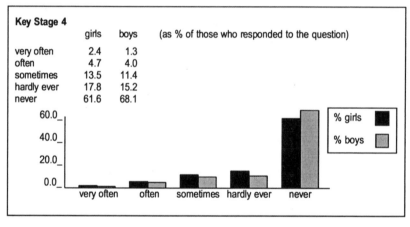

Key Stage 4

	girls	boys	(as % of those who responded to the question)
very often	2.4	1.3	
often	4.7	4.0	
sometimes	13.5	11.4	
hardly ever	17.8	15.2	
never	61.6	68.1	

Do you enjoy re-reading books your teacher has read with your class at school?

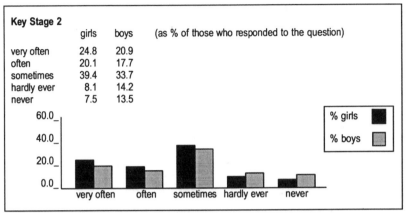

Key Stage 2

	girls	boys	(as % of those who responded to the question)
very often	24.8	20.9	
often	20.1	17.7	
sometimes	39.4	33.7	
hardly ever	8.1	14.2	
never	7.5	13.5	

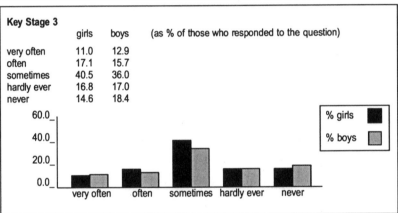

Key Stage 3

	girls	boys	(as % of those who responded to the question)
very often	11.0	12.9	
often	17.1	15.7	
sometimes	40.5	36.0	
hardly ever	16.8	17.0	
never	14.6	18.4	

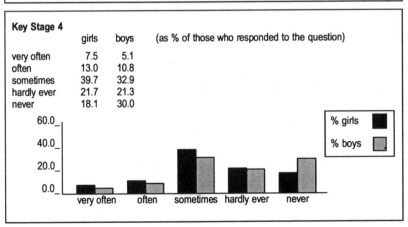

Key Stage 4

	girls	boys	(as % of those who responded to the question)
very often	7.5	5.1	
often	13.0	10.8	
sometimes	39.7	32.9	
hardly ever	21.7	21.3	
never	18.1	30.0	

If you BORROW books, how often do you borrow them from: Responses to the option: friends

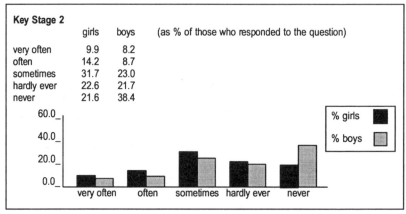

Key Stage 2

	girls	boys	(as % of those who responded to the question)
very often	9.9	8.2	
often	14.2	8.7	
sometimes	31.7	23.0	
hardly ever	22.6	21.7	
never	21.6	38.4	

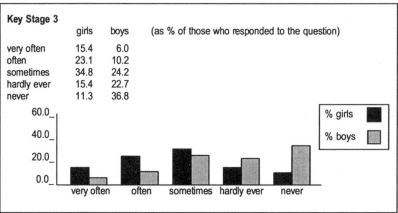

Key Stage 3

	girls	boys	(as % of those who responded to the question)
very often	15.4	6.0	
often	23.1	10.2	
sometimes	34.8	24.2	
hardly ever	15.4	22.7	
never	11.3	36.8	

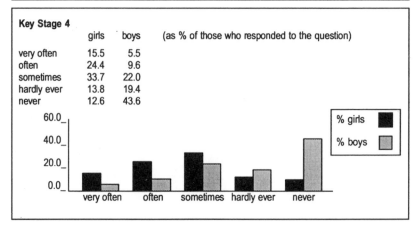

Key Stage 4

	girls	boys	(as % of those who responded to the question)
very often	15.5	5.5	
often	24.4	9.6	
sometimes	33.7	22.0	
hardly ever	13.8	19.4	
never	12.6	43.6	

If you BORROW books, how often do you borrow them from: Responses to the option: school library

Key Stage 2

	girls	boys	(as % of those who responded to the question)
very often	35.9	30.4	
often	25.6	21.5	
sometimes	22.3	22.6	
hardly ever	9.7	11.3	
never	6.4	14.3	

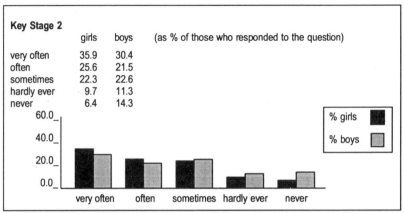

Key Stage 3

	girls	boys	(as % of those who responded to the question)
very often	26.9	23.9	
often	23.0	22.0	
sometimes	25.1	24.9	
hardly ever	15.2	14.4	
never	9.8	14.9	

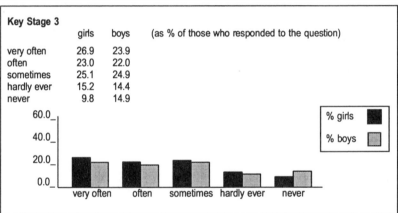

Key Stage 4

	girls	boys	(as % of those who responded to the question)
very often	9.2	8.2	
often	12.8	11.5	
sometimes	26.1	26.1	
hardly ever	29.7	23.4	
never	22.3	30.7	

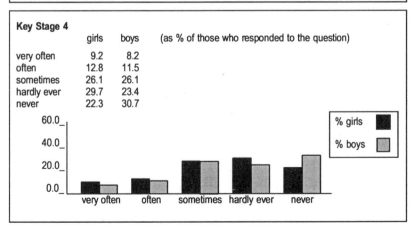

If you BORROW magazines, how often do you borrow them from: Responses to the option: friend(s)

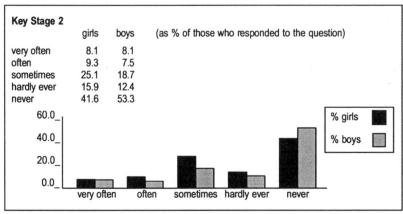

Key Stage 2

	girls	boys	(as % of those who responded to the question)
very often	8.1	8.1	
often	9.3	7.5	
sometimes	25.1	18.7	
hardly ever	15.9	12.4	
never	41.6	53.3	

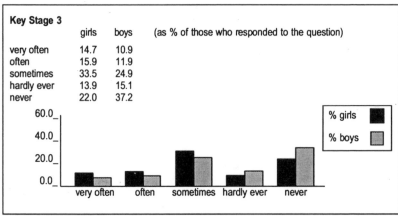

Key Stage 3

	girls	boys	(as % of those who responded to the question)
very often	14.7	10.9	
often	15.9	11.9	
sometimes	33.5	24.9	
hardly ever	13.9	15.1	
never	22.0	37.2	

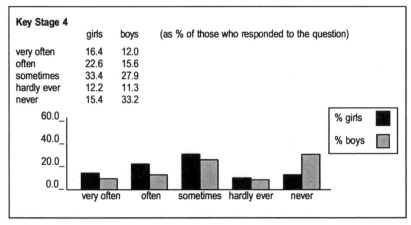

Key Stage 4

	girls	boys	(as % of those who responded to the question)
very often	16.4	12.0	
often	22.6	15.6	
sometimes	33.4	27.9	
hardly ever	12.2	11.3	
never	15.4	33.2	

How often do you choose a book because: Reponses to the option: it is about your hobby

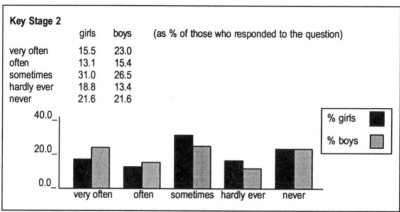

Key Stage 2

	girls	boys	(as % of those who responded to the question)
very often	15.5	23.0	
often	13.1	15.4	
sometimes	31.0	26.5	
hardly ever	18.8	13.4	
never	21.6	21.6	

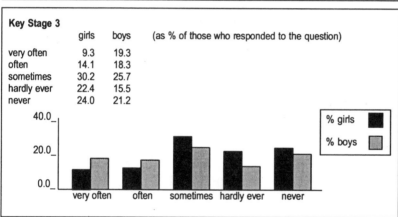

Key Stage 3

	girls	boys	(as % of those who responded to the question)
very often	9.3	19.3	
often	14.1	18.3	
sometimes	30.2	25.7	
hardly ever	22.4	15.5	
never	24.0	21.2	

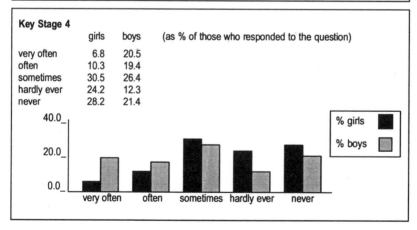

Key Stage 4

	girls	boys	(as % of those who responded to the question)
very often	6.8	20.5	
often	10.3	19.4	
sometimes	30.5	26.4	
hardly ever	24.2	12.3	
never	28.2	21.4	

**How often do you choose a book because: Responses to the option: the write-up ('blurb')
inside or on the cover makes it sound interesting**

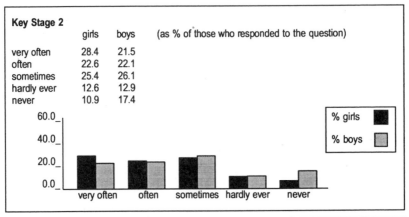

Key Stage 2

	girls	boys	(as % of those who responded to the question)
very often	28.4	21.5	
often	22.6	22.1	
sometimes	25.4	26.1	
hardly ever	12.6	12.9	
never	10.9	17.4	

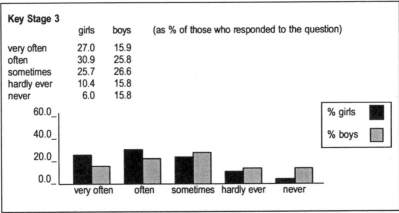

Key Stage 3

	girls	boys	(as % of those who responded to the question)
very often	27.0	15.9	
often	30.9	25.8	
sometimes	25.7	26.6	
hardly ever	10.4	15.8	
never	6.0	15.8	

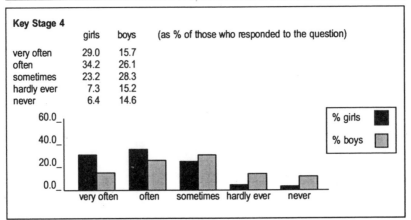

Key Stage 4

	girls	boys	(as % of those who responded to the question)
very often	29.0	15.7	
often	34.2	26.1	
sometimes	23.2	28.3	
hardly ever	7.3	15.2	
never	6.4	14.6	

How often do you choose a book because: Responses to the option: you like the look of the cover

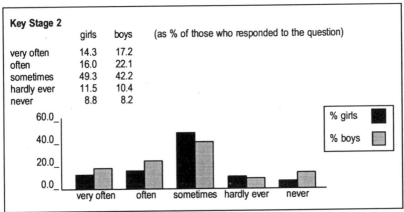

Key Stage 2

	girls	boys	(as % of those who responded to the question)
very often	14.3	17.2
often	16.0	22.1
sometimes	49.3	42.2
hardly ever	11.5	10.4
never	8.8	8.2

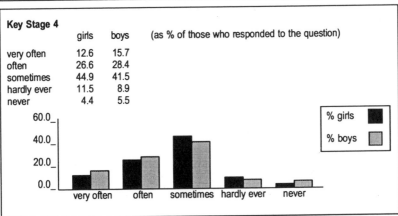

Key Stage 4

	girls	boys	(as % of those who responded to the question)
very often	12.6	15.7
often	26.6	28.4
sometimes	44.9	41.5
hardly ever	11.5	8.9
never	4.4	5.5

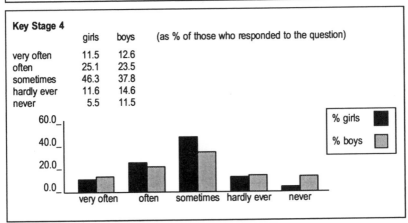

Key Stage 4

	girls	boys	(as % of those who responded to the question)
very often	11.5	12.6
often	25.1	23.5
sometimes	46.3	37.8
hardly ever	11.6	14.6
never	5.5	11.5

When you choose a book because of the look of the cover, is it because: Responses to the option: it looks up-to-date/modern

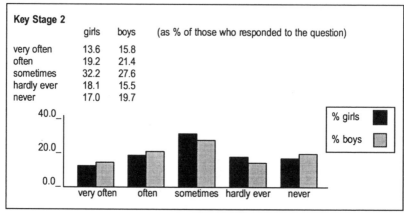

Key Stage 2

	girls	boys	(as % of those who responded to the question)
very often	13.6	15.8	
often	19.2	21.4	
sometimes	32.2	27.6	
hardly ever	18.1	15.5	
never	17.0	19.7	

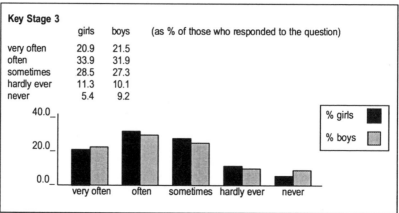

Key Stage 3

	girls	boys	(as % of those who responded to the question)
very often	20.9	21.5	
often	33.9	31.9	
sometimes	28.5	27.3	
hardly ever	11.3	10.1	
never	5.4	9.2	

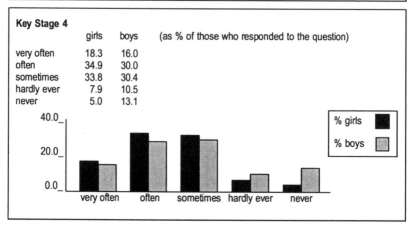

Key Stage 4

	girls	boys	(as % of those who responded to the question)
very often	18.3	16.0	
often	34.9	30.0	
sometimes	33.8	30.4	
hardly ever	7.9	10.5	
never	5.0	13.1	

How often do you choose a book because: Responses to the option: it is part of a series of the same sort of books

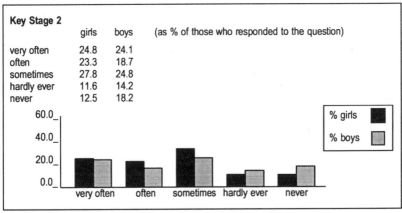

Key Stage 2

	girls	boys	(as % of those who responded to the question)
very often	24.8	24.1	
often	23.3	18.7	
sometimes	27.8	24.8	
hardly ever	11.6	14.2	
never	12.5	18.2	

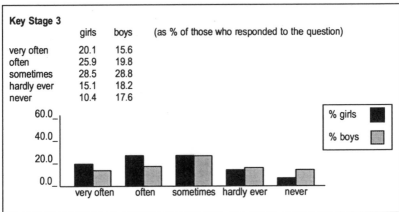

Key Stage 3

	girls	boys	(as % of those who responded to the question)
very often	20.1	15.6	
often	25.9	19.8	
sometimes	28.5	28.8	
hardly ever	15.1	18.2	
never	10.4	17.6	

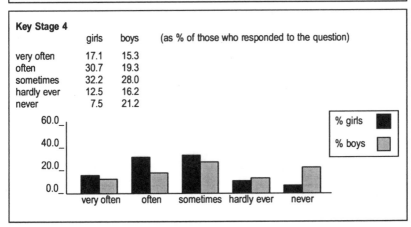

Key Stage 4

	girls	boys	(as % of those who responded to the question)
very often	17.1	15.3	
often	30.7	19.3	
sometimes	32.2	28.0	
hardly ever	12.5	16.2	
never	7.5	21.2	

When you choose books which are part of a series of similar types of books by the same publisher or author is it because: respondents who replied 'often' or 'very often' to the following options

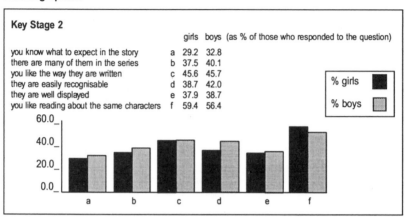

Key Stage 2

		girls	boys	(as % of those who responded to the question)
you know what to expect in the story	a	29.2	32.8	
there are many of them in the series	b	37.5	40.1	
you like the way they are written	c	45.6	45.7	
they are easily recognisable	d	38.7	42.0	
they are well displayed	e	37.9	38.7	
you like reading about the same characters	f	59.4	56.4	

% girls
% boys

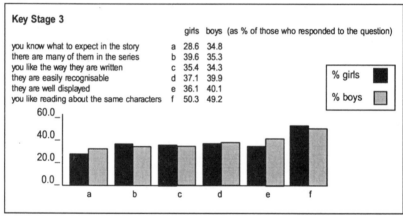

Key Stage 3

		girls	boys	(as % of those who responded to the question)
you know what to expect in the story	a	28.6	34.8	
there are many of them in the series	b	39.6	35.3	
you like the way they are written	c	35.4	34.3	
they are easily recognisable	d	37.1	39.9	
they are well displayed	e	36.1	40.1	
you like reading about the same characters	f	50.3	49.2	

% girls
% boys

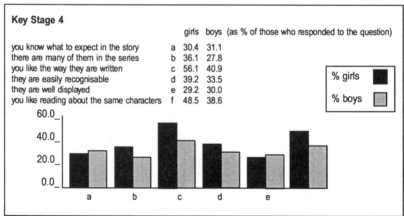

Key Stage 4

		girls	boys	(as % of those who responded to the question)
you know what to expect in the story	a	30.4	31.1	
there are many of them in the series	b	36.1	27.8	
you like the way they are written	c	56.1	40.9	
they are easily recognisable	d	39.2	33.5	
they are well displayed	e	29.2	30.0	
you like reading about the same characters	f	48.5	38.6	

% girls
% boys

How often do you read the following kinds of stories/fiction? Responses to the option: horror stories

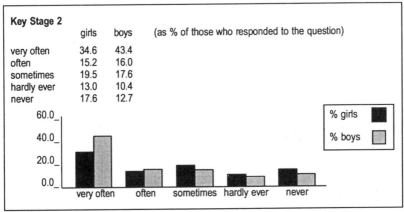

Key Stage 2

	girls	boys
very often	34.6	43.4
often	15.2	16.0
sometimes	19.5	17.6
hardly ever	13.0	10.4
never	17.6	12.7

(as % of those who responded to the question)

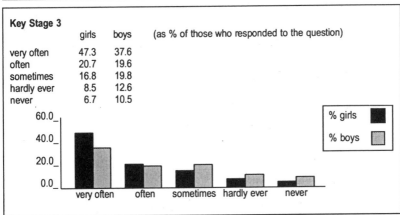

Key Stage 3

	girls	boys
very often	47.3	37.6
often	20.7	19.6
sometimes	16.8	19.8
hardly ever	8.5	12.6
never	6.7	10.5

(as % of those who responded to the question)

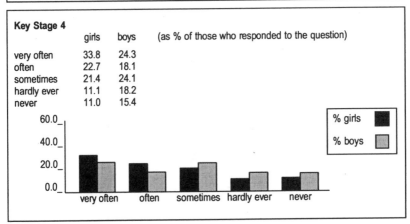

Key Stage 4

	girls	boys
very often	33.8	24.3
often	22.7	18.1
sometimes	21.4	24.1
hardly ever	11.1	18.2
never	11.0	15.4

(as % of those who responded to the question)

Books Mentioned by Children Taking Part in the Survey

KEY STAGE 2 – READING PREFERENCES

The range of books mentioned by the Key Stage 2 pupils interviewed is predictable with Roald Dahl, Enid Blyton and books in series featuring for both boys and girls. *Postman Pat* (John Cunliffe, published by Hippo Scholastic) remembered with affection. The range discussed is relatively wide, from Victorian adventure stories to 1950s classics and recent Smarties prize winners, such as Jacqueline Wilson. The girls, however, remembered more books that had been read in class than the boys. Both girls and boys mention, however, *The Hobbit* as being read in and out of school. It is quite surprising that this text is recalled, but it is a classic and opens up an amazing imaginary world for the reader, which obviously makes a strong impression on this age of pupil.

Girls

Private reading
Blyton, Enid *The Faraway Tree*: Mammoth
Blyton, Enid *The Adventures of the Wishing Chair*: Mammoth
Bond, Michael *Paddington*: HarperCollins
Dahl, Roald *Charlie and the Chocolate Factory*: Puffin
Dahl, Roald *Charlie and the Great Glass Elevator*: Puffin
Dahl, Roald *James and the Giant Peach*: Puffin
Dahl, Roald *The Twits*: Puffin
Dahl, Roald *Matilda*: Puffin
Fine, Anne *The Angel of Nitshill Road*: Mammoth Childrens
Frank, Anne *The Diary of Anne Frank*: Pan Paperback
Garner, Alan *Elidor*: Collins
Handford, Martin *Where's Wally?*: Walker
King-Smith, Dick *Lady Daisy*: Puffin

Norton, Mary *The Borrowers*: Puffin
Pearce, Philippa *What the Neighbours Did*: Puffin
Rosen, Michael *Hairy Tales & Nursery Crimes*: Puffin
Sommer-Bodenburg, Angela *The Little Vampire*: Scholastic
Stine, R. L. *The Curse of the Mummy's Tomb*: Scholastic
Tolkien, J. R. R. *The Hobbit*: Unwin Books
Wilson, Jacqueline *The Suitcase Kid*: Transworld

Series
Babysitters Club, various authors: Hippo/Scholastic
Point Horror, various authors: Hippo/Scholastic
St Clair, Enid Blyton: Hodder Children's
Famous Five, Enid Blyton: Hodder Children's
Secret Seven, Enid Blyton: Hodder Children's
Biggles, W. E. Johns: Arrow Red Fox
Nancy Drew, Carolyn Keene: HarperCollins

Class and school reading
Aiken, Joan *The Wolves of Willoughby Chase*: Puffin
Dahl, Roald *Charlie and the Chocolate Factory*: Puffin
Dahl, Roald *Matilda*: Puffin
Dahl, Roald *Boy*: Puffin
Carpenter, Humphrey *Mr Majeika*: Puffin
Hughes, Ted *The Iron Man*: Faber & Faber
Ingalls Wilder, Laura *Little House on the Prairie*: Mammoth
Lively, Penelope *QV66*: Mammoth
Lively, Penelope *A Stitch in Time*: Puffin
Mark, Jan *The Dead Letterbox*: Puffin
Morpurgo, Michael *Friend or Foe*: Mammoth
Serraillier, Ian *The Silver Sword*: Puffin
Tolkien, J. R. R. *The Hobbit*: Unwin Books
White, T. H. *The Sword in the Stone*: Collins

Boys

Private reading
Cooper, Susan *Dawn Wind*: Puffin
Dahl, Roald *Charlie and the Chocolate Factory*: Puffin
Hardcastle, John *Penalty*: Orion Children
Jacques, Brian *The Redwall Stories*: Arrow Fed Fox

Kastner, Eric *Emile and the Detectives*: Red Fox
Margorian, Michelle *Goodnight Mr Tom*: Puffin
Pearce, Phillippa *Tom's Midnight Garden*: Puffin
Serraillier, Ian *The Silver Sword*: Puffin
Shakespeare, William *Hamlet*
Stevenson, Robert Louis *Treasure Island*: Puffin
Stevenson, Robert Louis *Kidnapped*: Puffin
Tolkien, J. R. R. *The Hobbit*: Unwin Books
Tolkien, J. R. R. *The Lord of the Rings*: Unwin Books
Tolkien, J. R. R. *Farmer Giles of Ham*: Unwin Books

Series
Point Horror, various authors: Hippo/Scholastic
Famous Five, Enid Blyton: Hodder Children's
The Hardy Boys, W. Dixon: HarperCollins
Asterix, Goscinny & Uderzo: Hodder
Biggles, W. E. Johns: Arrow Red Fox
Nancy Drew, Carolyn Keene: HarperCollins
Goosebumps, R. L. Stine: Hippo/Scholastic

Class and school reading
Cameron, Ann *Julian Secret Agent*: Transworld
Carpenter, Humphrey *The Conjuror's Game*: Puffin
Dahl, Roald *George's Marvellous Medicine*: Puffin
Jones, Terry *The Saga of Eric the Viking*: Puffin
Serraillier, Ian *The Silver Sword*: Puffin
Tolkien, J. R. R. *The Hobbit*: Unwin Books

KEY STAGE 3 – READING PREFERENCES

It is not surprising to find that in the interviews, girls of this age had more to say about their private reading than the boys. Nearly twice as many books were named by the girls and the range of their reading is wider. The only title in common is Townsend's *The Secret Diary of Adrian Mole aged 13³/₄* and this was recalled enthusiastically by several interviewees. The class reading lists include books which were not always remembered affectionately. For example, Betsy Byars's *The Midnight Fox* was described as boring by several 11 and 12 year olds. In contrast, Janni Howker's *The Nature of The Beast* and Nigel Hinton's *Buddy* were described as good choices.

Girls

Private reading
Adams, D *The Hitchhiker's Guide to the Galaxy*: Pan
Anderson, R. *The War Orphan*: Richard Drew
Awdry, C. *Thomas the Tank Engine*: Reed
Blume, J. *Tiger Eyes*: Pan
Cooney, C. *Saturday Night*: Hippo/Scholastic
Crichton, M. *Jurassic Park*: Random House
Dahl, Roald *George's Marvellous Medicine*: Puffin
Dahl, Roald *Boy*: Puffin
Dahl, Roald *Matilda*: Puffin
Dickinson, M. *Alex Books*: Hippo/Scholastic
Filipovic, Z. *Zlata's Diary*: Puffin
Fine, A. *Madame Doubtfire*: Puffin
Fine, A. *Goggle Eyes*: Puffin
Harris, T. *The Silence of the Lambs*: Mandarin
Harvey/McKenna, *Headlines from the Jungle*: Puffin
Hinton, N. *Beaver Towers*: Puffin
Horse, H. *The Last Polar Bears*: Puffin
Jarvis, R. *Whitby Series*: Macdonald Young Books
King, S. *Misery*: Hodder & Stoughton
Lingard, J. *Across the Barricades*: Puffin
Pilgrim, Jane *Blackberry Farm*: Hodder & Stoughton
Serraillier, I. *The Silver Sword*: Puffin
Sewell, A. *Black Beauty*: Puffin
Stine, R. L. *The Hitchhiker*: Hippo/Scholastic
Swindells, R. *Stone Cold*: Puffin
Townsend, S. *The Secret Diary of Adrian Mole aged 13³/₄*: Mandarin
Trollope, J. *The Rector's Wife*: Corgi
Voight, C. *Homecoming*: HarperCollins

Class and school reading
Baldwin, M. *Grandad with Snails* (out of print)
Bawden, N. *Carrie's War*: Puffin
Byars, B. *The Midnight Fox*: Puffin
Cross, Gillian *The Dark Behind The Curtain*: Hippo/Scholastic
Dahl, Roald *Boy*: Puffin
Dahl, Roald *The Wonderful World of Henry Sugar*: Puffin
Hinton, N. *Buddy*: Puffin

Howker, J. *The Nature of the Beast*: HarperCollins
Lingard, J. *Across The Barricades*: Puffin
Pearce, P. *Tom's Midnight Garden*: Puffin

Series
Babysitters Club, various authors: Hippo/Scholastic
Famous Five, Enid Blyton: Hodder Children's
Malory Towers, Enid Blyton: Bounty
Point Horror, various authors: Hippo/Scholastic
Sweet Valley High, Francine Pascell: Transworld Children's
The Boyfriend Club, Janet Quin-Harkin: Puffin

Boys

Private reading
Brickhill, P. *The Dam Busters*: Pan
Cooney, C. *The Stranger*: Hippo/Scholastic
Dahl, R. *The Wonderful World of Henry Sugar*: Puffin
Fine, A. *Madame Doubtfire*: Puffin
Hinton, N. *Beaver Towers*: Puffin
Johns, Capt. W. E. *Biggles*: Red Fox
Lawrence, L. *Children of The Dust*: Red Fox
Pike, C. *The Last Act*: Hodder & Stoughton
Stevenson, R. L. *Kidnapped*: Puffin
Swindells, R. *Brother in the Land*: Puffin
Townsend, S. *The Secret Diary of Adrian Mole aged 13³/₄*: Mandarin
Westall, R. *The Machine Gunners*: Pan

Class and school reading
Byars, B. *The Eighteenth Emergency*: Puffin
Byars, B. *The Midnight Fox*: Puffin
Christopher, J. *The Guardians*: Puffin
Dahl, Roald *Boy*: Puffin
Garfield, L. *Black Jack*: Puffin
Hinton, N. *Buddy*: Puffin
Holm, A. *I am David*: Mammoth
Laird, E. *Red Sky in the Morning*: Piper
Mark, J. *Thunder and Lightnings*: Puffin
Serraillier, I. *The Silver Sword*: Puffin

KEY STAGE 4 – READING PREFERENCES

The range of independent reading mentioned by boys and girls of this age is wide. The lists for both sexes include adult fiction titles as well as books written for younger children. Books from a series do not feature so prominently with this age group. Several pre-twentieth century titles are being read by girls while boys cite autobiographies. Very few texts studied in schools were named although reading in school was discussed. Their comments are considered in Chapter 2.

Girls

Private reading
Alcott, L. M. *Little Women*: Puffin
Blume, J. *Forever*: Pan
Blume, J. *Are You There God? It's Me Margaret*: Pan
Brontë, C. *Jane Eyre*: Puffin
Dickens, C. *A Christmas Carol*: Puffin
Dickens C. *Great Expectations*: Puffin
Dickens C. *Oliver Twist*: Puffin
Fry, S. *The Liar*: Mandarin
Graham, K. *The Wind in the Willows*: Puffin
Kesey, K. *One Flew Over the Cuckoo's Nest*: Pan
Montgomery, L. M. *Anne of Green Gables*: Puffin
Plath, S. *The Bell Jar*: Faber & Faber
Thackeray, W. *Vanity Fair*:
Townsend, S. *The Queen and I*: Mandarin

Class and school reading
Hines, B. A. *A Kestrel for a Knave*: Penguin
Miller, A. *A View From the Bridge*: Heinemann Educational
Priestley, J. B. *An Inspector Calls*: Heinemann Educational
Shakespeare, W. *Macbeth*
Williams, T. *A Streetcar Named Desire*: Methuen

Series
Point Horror, various authors: Hippo/Scholastic
Sweet Dreams, various authors: Transworld

Boys

Private reading
Botham I, *Botham – My Autobiography*: HarperCollins
Breslin, T. *Kezzie*: Mammoth
Elton, B. *Stark*: Warner
Golding, W. *The Lord of the Flies*: Faber & Faber
Harris, T. *The Silence of the Lambs*: Mandarin
Higgins, J. *The Eagle Has Landed*: Pan
Kerouac, J. *On The Road*: Penguin
Lively, P. *The Ghost of Thomas Kemp*: Mammoth
Marten, N. *Freddie Mercury & Queen*: Penguin
Pike, C. *Die Softly*: Hodder
Townsend, S. *The Secret Diary of Adrian Mole aged 13³/₄*: Mandarin

Class and school reading
Hinton, N. *Buddy*: Puffin
O'Brien, R. *Z for Zachariah*: HarperCollins
Shakespeare, W. *Macbeth*

Bibliography

Appleyard, J. A. (1990) *Becoming a Reader. The Experience of Fiction from Childhood to Adulthood.* Cambridge: Cambridge University Press.

Barrs, M. *et al.* (1989) *The Primary Language Record Handbook for Teachers.* London: ILEA/CLPE.

Barrs, M. & Thomas, A. (eds) (1991) *The Reading Book.* London: CLPE.

Beard, R. (1990) *Developing Reading.* London: Hodder & Stoughton.

Bennett, D. (1995) *Books for Keeps.* Issue 90, January.

Benton, M. & Fox, G. (1985) *Teaching Literature – Nine to Fourteen.* Oxford: Oxford University Press.

Carey, J. 'Rip off their jackets and get the joy of texts', London: *The Guardian* 4/4/97.

Chambers, A. (1985) *Booktalk Occasional Writing on Literature and Children.* London: Bodley Head.

Chambers, A. (1991) *The Reading Environment.* Glos: Thimble Press.

Chambers, A. (1993) *Tell Me. Children Talk, Reading & Talk.* Glos. Thimble Press.

Chandler, D. & Marcus, S. (1981) *Computers and Literacy.* Milton Keynes: Open University Press.

Cox, B. (1991) *Cox on Cox, An English Curriculum for the 1990s.* London: Hodder & Stoughton.

Creaser, C. (1995) *A Survey of Library Services to Schools and Children in the UK 1994–5.* Loughborough: Loughborough University of Technology.

DfE (1995) *English in the National Curriculum.* London: HMSO.

Fox, Geoff (ed.) (1976) *Writers, Critics & Children.* London: Heinemann.

Gorman, T. P. (1987) Pupils' Attitudes to Reading at Age 11 and 15. APU Survey, Windsor NFER: Nelson.

Gorman, T. P. White, J. *et al.* (1988) *Language Performance in Schools: a review of APU Language Monitoring 1979 – 1983.* London: DES.

HMI (1990) *The Teaching and Learning of Reading in Primary Schools.* London: DES.

Hunt, P. (1993) 'Finding the Right Book for a Reader', in *The Power of the Page*, Pinsent, P. (ed.) London: Fulton Press.

Inglis, F. (1981) *The Promise of Happiness*. Cambridge: Cambridge University Press.

King, C. & Robinson, M. 'Creating Communities of Readers in English in Education', Volume 20 No. 2 National Association for the Teaching of English (NATE).

Meek, M. (1991) *On Being Literate*. London: Bodley Head.

OFSTED (1993) *Boys and English: A Report from the Office of Her Majesty's Inspector for Schools (HMI)*. London: DfE.

Phillips, A. (1993) *The Trouble with Boys, Parenting the Men for the Future*. London: Pandora.

Pinsent, P. (ed.) (1993) *The Power of the Page*. London: Fulton Press.

Pugh, K. (1995) 'Boys and English: Classroom Voices', in *The English and Media Magazine* No. 33, London: English and Media Centre.

Reynolds, K. (ed.) (1994) *Contemporary Juvenile Reading Habits: A study of young people's reading at the end of the century*. London: British Library.

Reynonds, K. (ed.) (1996) *Young People's Reading at the End of the Century*. London: Book Trust, British Library Report No. 14.

Sarland, Charles (1991) *Young People's Reading: Culture and Response*. Milton Keynes: Open University Press.

Sarland, C. (1994) 'Attack of the Teenage Horrors: Theme and Meaning in Popular Series Fiction' Glos: *Signal*.

SCAA (1995) 'One week in March: a survey of the literature pupils read' SCAA discussion papers No. 4, London: SCAA publications.

Southgate, V. *et al*. (1981) *Extending Beginning Reading*. London: Heinemann.

Tucker, N. (1981) *The Child and the Book. A Psychological and Literary Exploration*. Cambridge: Cambridge University Press.

Weidemann, K. (1969) *Book Jackets & Record Sleeves*. London: Thames & Hudson.

Other sources

Educational Publishers' Council

Library and Information Services Council/Statistics Unit Loughborough

Library Association

Bookbird/IBBY

Index

Appleyard, J., 69, 71
Assessment of Performance Unit, 40

Bedtime stories, 21–23
Benton, M. & Fox, G., 18
Biography, 47
Blume, Judy, 6, 33, 43
Blyton, Enid, 8, 28, 69, 72
Bookclubs, 57
Bookcover blurbs, 52, 63, 66
Books for Keeps, 60, 71
Bookjackets, 47
Bookshops, 30, 58–9
Book titles, 67

Chambers, A., 4, 9, 23, 25, 30
Class Readers, 3, 15, 17
CD Rom, 9, 55
Comics, 37, 39, 47
Cox, B., 11

Dickinson, P., 29

English for ages 5–16 (1989), 22
English in the National
   Curriculum (1995), 3, 4, 5, 7, 8,
   9, 19
English teachers, 11, 18, 19, 29, 36,
   45, 78

Fathers, 30, 31

GCSE, 15, 34, 46
Gender differences, 7, 34, 37, 39
Grandmothers, 31–2
Graphic novels, 47
Group reading, 36

Health & sexuality, 43
Hobbit, The, by J. R. R. Tolkien,
   23, 26, 28

Inglis, F., 72

Librarians, 35, 47, 52
Libraries:
   Public libraries, 27, 47, 50–3, 67
   School libraries, 8, 35, 53–6
Library funding, 54

Meek, M., 21
Midnight Fox, The, by Betsy
   Byars, 4, 6, 12
Mothers, 26–30

National Centre for Research in
   Children's Literature, The
   (NCRCL), 1
National Curriculum, 40

OFSTED, 39–40
One Week in March SCAA Report,
   6, 16, 19

Peer Pressure, 43, 45

Pickard, P. M., 73

Pinsent, P., 8

Plowden Report, The (1966), 49

Point Horror, 13, 66, 71, 72, 73, 74

Primary class teachers, 3, 5, 7, 9

Questionnaire, The, 86

Reading aloud, 4

Reading as a hobby, 76, 80

Reading difficulties, 77–8

Reading for information, 9, 43

Sarland, C., 74

School bookshops, 57

Shared reading, 45

Teaching and Learning of Reading in Primary Schools, The, HMI Report, 3

Teen magazines, 37, 42

Television, 25, 31, 33, 51, 79

Tom's Midnight Garden by Philippa Pearce, 13–14

Young People's Reading at the End of the Century (Survey) (1996), 1, 7, 26, 30, 33–4, 36, 37, 42, 49–50, 63, 64, 72, 73